WORTH IT ALL

The most prized thing in God's eyes

Wouter van der Westhuizen

First Published 2024 by Wouter van der Westhuizen
Copyright © 2024 Wouter van der Westhuizen

ISBN 978-0-7961-3957-3 (Print)
ISBN 978-0-7961-3958-0 (eBook)

Cover and interior crafted with love by the team at
www.myebook.online

MYEBOOK
WE EMPOWER AUTHORS

Contents

Preface

The idea for this book came out of some research I was doing for another book I was writing, called *The Expectation Gap*, which centres on the wisdom of God we need to apply in our everyday lives. In my research, I realised how great an impact misplaced expectations can have on the lives of individuals or even nations. Our wrong perceptions of others and situations can have disastrous consequences in our lives.

I kept pondering the reasons and results of the gaps between people's expectations of each other and their reality. My studies considered relationships in the business world – analysing the impact of the gap in expectations between a buyer and seller – and I found the gap to be responsible for great losses. This led me to conclude that the effect of the gap in people's expectations comes down to an area I call critical resources. Before a product is sold, shipped, produced, or even designed, a critical resource is created – which is the relationship between two parties; in this case between a buyer and seller. I isolated this bond and found that it is *the* critical resource, and so I began looking at relationships as a foundation stone, which not only has bearing on our earthly lives, bat also on our lives beyond our life on earth.

The most precious resource humanity has is our relationships. This critical resource enables us to either enjoy life to the full, or to make a life resembling a litany of disasters. I concluded that if the relationship between human beings is such a key aspect, then how much more important is our relationship with God?

Imagine the joy when two people get married. Imagine the pain when they get divorced. It is all due to the gap in their expectations of each other. Imagine too, the pain and suffering for the rest of their lives. Now take this further; imagine what pain and regret we would suffer if our assumptions regarding heaven were wrong. Imagine dying and God refusing us entry into Paradise. Wouldn't we suffer unimaginable pain if we were to realise at the point of death that we misunderstood what God had expected of us. Standing at the gates of heaven and being prevented from entering, we would wonder what we had missed. What did we do wrong? Or perhaps – what did we not do that resulted in this? We would come to the bitter conclusion that we neglected the most valuable thing in life – a relationship with God. This is the most precious thing we need to cultivate here on earth.

WOUTER VAN DER WESTHUIZEN

Introduction

Have you ever asked yourself what mankind's most precious possession is? Then ask yourself if that possession is also precious to God? Can we take this possession with us into the life hereafter? What in this world is so important that people are willing to die for? What in this world is worth giving up my all for? What becomes sweeter as it grows? Is there something in this life, something so precious, that I am willing to die for it?

I have written this book with two specific purposes in mind.

Firstly, in my years of being a pastor and having seen many people getting saved, I have always pondered the journey God took the nation of Israel on. Was His plan of salvation a single event that would lead to their freedom? Or was it meant to be a process to build a relationship between Israel and their God? My studies made me investigate if we perhaps sometimes sell salvation as a cheap 'insurance policy' and not as an eternal relationship with God. I began looking into what Scripture reveals regarding true joy – I wanted to know if it is achievable in this life. As I studied true joy, all the aspects of false joy started emerging and I began asking questions: when God set Israel free from Egyptian slavery, did He stop there, or did He have more in mind for them? Was His intention for Israel a joy based on their freedom from slavery, or was it a joy resulting from true rest; an inheritance and a daily relationship with Him?

Secondly, as I read Genesis, I see God creating a home and people to live in it with Him. I see Him walking with His people as His family in a beautiful garden with rivers and trees. Sadly, I see how man fell into sin, which caused humanity to struggle as they carved out an existence apart from God. Later on, Scripture shows how God walked with Abraham, Isaac, Joseph, Moses, and the nation of Israel. And many years later, Jesus is born to restore the relationship between God and man. When turning to the book of Revelation at the end of the Bible, I see what was in the beginning in Genesis: I see a beautiful garden with rivers and trees and God walking with His people.

When these two aspects are combined, a theme emerges in Scripture – we see God building a relationship with His people. I have lived with burning questions in my heart in my Christian life for many years. Through many trials, as all people undergo, I started to answer some of these questions. I became convinced that it is worth foregoing everything this world can offer. I have seen what lies ahead and why the devil is so busy, as he himself acknowledged to God in the book of Job chapter 1. I have seen what keeps us busy and why there is nothing this world can offer that can compare with what is kept for us after we leave this life.

As I explored Scripture through the eyes of a relational God, who, from the beginning of Scripture to the end and beyond, wants to be with the people He loves, I began studying what it means to reciprocate the love we have received.

As an example, not long ago I walked into a business premises and was greeted by a young woman who asked if she could help me. From the front desk I could see and hear what was happening in the offices behind her. I heard the voice of a little boy, a toddler, who was pulling items off the desks. The young woman called out: "Mom, would you please help there before he breaks something." I asked if he was her little boy, at which she smiled and said: "Yes, my first one."

Then the front door opened and an older man entered. He gave the young girl a quick smile and walked directly into the offices. What he said next explained who he was and why he was there. He said: "Where's my little boy?" I asked the young woman if that was her father. She laughed and said, yes, he was the little boy's grandfather, and that her father now only came to work to play with his grandson – the child was all he was interested in. The grandfather was an accomplished businessman, but now, nearing retirement, life had become dull and empty. He had realised that money cannot buy true joy, and he had found joy and worth in his family – and especially in his little grandson.

This real-life illustration highlights that the most precious thing we have, the thing that outshines the biggest diamond, is our relationships with others. If we begin to understand how vitally important our relationships with each other are for our wellbeing, then our focus will turn to how eternally important our relationship with God is. He is the One who created us in His own image and likeness; the One who sustains us by His eternal life and grace; the One who loves us and gave Himself as a ransom to set us free from sin and death.

How to read this book

This book is built around a central theme, which I trust will have an impact on the lives of many believers.

As with Scripture, this book presents God as the main character. He is the Creator of the universe and everything in it, and He created mankind according to His likeness and in His own image. Mankind is a sub-character in this book, which shows how they spend their days looking for God, or looking for themselves in God. It is this seeking after God that develops as a key theme.

This overarching theme details the value of man's relationship with God and each other. The ever-growing myriad of distractions offered by the world to keep people from getting to know God personally is the conflict raging in every person. Satan himself is behind these temptations and distractions. He entices every person along the lines of their own weaknesses and brokenness. Mankind has to wage war to rise above what the world offers and see what God has planned for those who diligently seek Him. The setting, relevant to mankind, is the earth and the spiritual war that rages in the heavenlies for mankind's worship, focus, time, and devotion (souls).

The development of healthy relationships with those around us is of secondary importance. Before we do this, we are to develop a personal relationship with our heavenly Father, which is mediated by Jesus Christ, His Son. This is the primary relationship we are to develop. While Jesus mediates salvation to the believer, the Holy Spirit develops our fellowship with God.

The flow of this book begins with looking at how aspects such as obedience, love and trust are not only crucial to any relationship, but are intricately interwoven into the framework of any relationship. Scripture, which is God's relational instruction manual to mankind, forms a major part of this book. The rest of the book contains thought-provoking aspects regarding our relationships with God and others. Each discussion item, in the form of a chapter, has a direct link to relationships and can be expanded. Some of these discussion items will question the reader's ideologies, beliefs and practices.

The aim of this book is to influence the reader to consider making changes after weighing up the value of our relationships compared with so many activities busying our everyday lives. I do, presumptuously, assume that every believer has a personal relationship with God. I therefore set out to present a book that can convince both believer and non-believer that putting God first is truly worth it all.

Part One

In the beginning God

Chapter 1

What are relationships?

A relationship is where two or more people are linked by a bond through the giving and receiving of tangible or non-tangible things to each other, in a specific context over a period of time. This bond can be established through common ground or it may be centred around something shared.

The parties need not be equal in power, status, position or prominence. A relationship can exist between a king and a poor man, and it does not have to benefit both parties. It can exist between business partners, friends, families, affiliations, spouses, and many more. What sets them apart are the different levels in which love is expressed – 'love' in this instance represents ways of expressing closeness or intimacy. Intimacy is not limited to the sexuality, nor is intimacy limited to humanity and love is not always what God designed it to be.

Sociology explains that humans are social beings who need to relate to each other, to be in relationships where people touch each other, converse, and connect with each other. People need people. This is how God created us. We are relational beings just as He is. After all, we have been made in His image and likeness. When people are isolated, they become depressed. People need to be close, and closeness does not necessarily refer to physical touch or affection. Whether a relationship exists between all humans sharing the same original ancestor, Adam, or a link between two or more people gathered around a business idea, or a platonic relationship between two friends; or the physical and emotional intimacy reserved for marriage – all relationships originate from God, and His Word contains guidelines for them all.

God's love at the heart of relationships

God Himself is the author and initiator of the principle of relationships. God is love and He does not create anything that does not flow out of His nature – love is the key element that should underpin the nature of any relationship. Love is always expressed in a place of peace and freedom, and in a willingness to give and receive.

Paul explains in 1 Corinthians 13 that love is never self-seeking, proud and it always chooses truth. Love always considers what is best for the other person. When exploring love, we should not use the examples of broken relationships we see in this fallen world. God is the source of all relationships, but when His loving nature is removed from a relationship, we are left with wilful deceit, and misuse and abuse of each other. God is not the author of abuse – Satan is. In Genesis we see how Satan broke into the principle of the relationship God created and introduced pride, rebellion, selfishness, deceit and hate. He removed love – and in doing so, he sowed seeds of distrust, abuse, and all the societal ills we see today.

When we look at the definition and inner workings of a true relationship, we acknowledge that only God can be its designer and author. No other aspect in the universe is so complex, so fulfilling, and on which so much hinges. The inverse is also true. When we attempt to remove the principle of love in relationships, we find ourselves arguing against the wisdom and nature of God. God embodies love, which is seen in patience, joy, forgiveness, reconciliation, trust, truth, humility, grace, meekness, unity and holiness. The opposite attributes to these point directly to the enemy of God – the devil. His purpose is to separate, to bring disunity, hatred, deceit, lies, anger, death, and destruction. What God has created, the devil intrudes and distorts. For this reason, we see a world full of broken relationships – from individual level through to nations warring against each other.

A relationship can only be found where a living being has the ability to relate to God as a Spirit. A relationship cannot exist between humans and objects. Humans are the only beings in God's earthly creation who have the Spirit of God in them and who, through the Spirit, can respond to God.

Furthermore, love, which is the essence of a godly relationship, requires the Spirit to first understand God, and then to respond to His love. It is therefore clear that man can only find true love and joy in relationships with each other and with God. No relationship can be established with a cold dead object, such as carved images, where no love can be given or received.. This is a perversion of God's ordained boundaries for mankind.

From Genesis to Revelation, Scripture reveals God's autobiography. Throughout the sixty-six books of the Bible, the divine Creator is saying He wants to dwell with the people He loves. Scripture introduces us to the love story of a Father who wants to be with His children – a Father who will stop at nothing to make this possible. This same narrative is repeated several times in Scripture. We see how the incarnated Jesus comes to earth and pays the ultimate price to reconcile God's children back to Him. It is the greatest love story ever told.

The Scriptural pattern of God present among His people originates from the Genesis account of creation where God walked with Adam and Eve. The first two people on earth were created by God for God and they walked with God. Later on, God's people fell away on account of sin, but after some time, God again built the relationship with someone He called His friend. It was Abraham.

Through Abraham and the trust he placed in God, a new people of God was established. In Exodus 3:7, God says He heard the cries of Abraham's children when they were caught in Egyptian slavery. This was the Jewish people, the descendants of Abraham whom God called His chosen people. God powerfully delivered Israel from slavery so they could become a royal nation – a people belonging to Him. This pattern continues from the Old Testament into the New Testament where the church, the New Israel of God (Galatians 6:16), Jews and Gentiles, is established to be the people of God forever. In both the Old and New Testaments, we see a chosen people with whom God chooses to dwell.

Understanding sin

It is necessary for us to have a meaningful understanding of sin. The word 'sin' spells disaster for any relationship. Whether the relationship is with God or among mankind, 'sin' is poison in a relationship. It destroys it. Sin can be embodied in many different thoughts and actions, and it targets relationships of every kind.

The core fact of sin is that it removes a person's righteousness, which means to be in right-standing with God. All sin is committed against God Himself. We see what happened to Adam in Genesis 3 when he fell into sin. The effect was instantaneous – Adam and his wife lost their right-standing with God and were banished from the Garden of Eden. Sin caused man's removal from God's sustaining presence.

Sin is the opposite of holiness, and because God is eternally holy, whatever is tainted with sin must be removed from His presence. Sin is by nature irrational, because it leads to the removal of a person from God's sustaining eternal life – and eventual death. This is what Adam and Even found out after they disobeyed God; apart from God, their bodies started to decay and their lives became a testimony of mere survival, not triumph. They lost the innocence and purity they had when they walked with God. The only way their relationship with God could be restored was for sin to be removed.

Throughout Scripture, from Genesis to Revelation, a few major themes are found in its meta-narrative. If the main purpose of Scripture is to glorify God, then the main theme of Scripture is reconciliation. Why is reconciliation needed, and why is the theme of bringing back together what was lost such an important aspect in Scripture? In many churches around the world, salvation is preached with reference to the cross of Christ, God's grace, faith, and other related topics. However, we don't often teach on the power of sin; what it is, where it comes from, and what its effects are. Although temptation is mentioned on a regular basis during sermons, Scripture teaches us in James 1 that temptation is merely one of the steps relating to sin. It is important to see what causes sin, because it has had an effect on all of humanity past, present and future (Romans 5:12). Sin is the one single deciding factor for every human being between eternal life (heaven) or death (hell).

God's song of reconciliation

The power of sin is death, which caused God to act to undo sin's power. If sin causes God Himself to step in, then we need to know why God acted in such a pivotal way. Scripture points this out in no uncertain terms. In Matthew 1:21 we read that Jesus came to save His people from their sin. Jesus' entrance into mankind's existence in the New Testament was primarily to deal decisively with sin and its effects. It was God's focus from Genesis 3:15 until Jesus was born in Bethlehem. Dealing with sin meant that the relationship between man and God could be re-established. Said another way; after sin is removed, the relationship between God and man can be restored.

This points to two important facts. Firstly, Jesus died on the cross so we can again be God's friends (1 Peter 3:18). Secondly, the restored friendship with God that we are now privileged to have, opens the door to all God's blessings, favour and promises. These could not have been ours, despite many who ignorantly claim them, without an established relationship with God. Throughout this book this principle is repeated: God gave His all to save us all. The relationship He has called us into is worth it all.

The origin of relationships

God is the Creator of all and sustains everything by His Word and power. Scripture tells us that God exists in a relationship as the Trinity. Everything God does or creates emanates from and operates within the boundary of the relationship within the Trinity.

What this means is when God creates something, it is designed to fit within the boundaries of authority He has assigned to it. While animals live in social structures, humans live in a special framework God has assigned to them. We function within relationships, with each other and with God, as He designed it. Whether in families, villages, towns and cities, humans were created to be in relationships. What is key to all God created, is that they were created to relate to God in some way.

Mankind is a created being and is not the author or designer of the principle of a relationship. When we consider this, we will find that God has placed His principle of relationships within our nature. It is this part of our nature that allows the functioning of love. How else can we understand when Scripture says in 1 John 4:16: "God is love." When we read 1 John chapters 1-4, we begin to see how John highlights the fact that God is love. He stresses that love comes from God and that love exists within us as we relate to each other. For love to exist and function, it needs the context of a relationship. Therefore, without the aspect of a relationship, we cannot understand the giving and receiving of love. In the introduction to his book, the apostle John speaks of "fellowship", of "us," "our" and "your." He is saying that what he has seen, heard, touched, and learnt, he did so while being in fellowship with others and with God. His greatest desire is that this fellowship with God and others will spread to everyone.

It is worth noting how God structured relationships at the time of creation. The relationship between Adam (human) and God (divine) is called a vertical relationship. The relationships between humans – between friends or a husband and wife – are called horizontal relationships. Both vertical and horizontal relationships are a clear picture of how God purposely created mankind and how He desires things should work.

9

Having considered the fall of mankind into sin, we can see that it caused people to be alienated from the presence and fellowship of God. This means that the relationships between God and man, and between man and man were broken. The key narrative running throughout Scripture is that of reconciliation, depicting the restoration of a broken relationship. It refers to the restoration of the friendship between God and man, and between all mankind. It is not surprising then that God's song in Scripture centres around the restoration of the relationship between Himself and the people He created. Throughout this book, relationships are presented as the most prized thing in God's eyes. God's hymn of loving reconciliation throughout the ages sounds from His heavenly throne and is embodied in His Son's coming to earth to atone for mankind's sinful rebellion. Every sinner saved daily is a sign of God's continuing work of grace and love to reconcile man to Himself.

Throughout Scripture the building, development and restoration of relationships is a key theme. From the Old Testament prophets, whose purpose was to call the people of God back to Him, to the twelve apostles in the New Testament, who, together with every believer alive today, were given the charge by Jesus Himself to be ambassadors of God's plan of reconciliation (2 Corinthians 5:11-21). From Genesis to Revelation, throughout the ages, we see how God tirelessly pursues the restoration of His relationship with mankind. His constant pursuit is the friendship between Himself and humans.

God's instructions for relationships

In His Sermon on the Mount (Matthew 5:1-10), Jesus explained the ways of God to the listeners who sat around Him. His sermon that day was also intended for us today. He gave instructions to us, not only on how to be His loyal followers, but how to build a relationship with God and with our neighbour. The instructions He gave were not His own, but those of His Father in heaven. What Jesus explained were not rigid laws, but principles on how to establish and maintain relationships. These principles are in line with what Matthew says in Matthew 1:21 (NIV): "She will give birth to a son, and you are to give him the name Jesus, because he will save his people from their sins."

The key issue regarding sin is that it separates man from the sustaining presence, life, and peace of God. While Satan is the cause of this separation, Jesus came to undo what Satan caused. Jesus was crucified, died and was raised so He could reconcile people back to God. Jesus' sacrificial death ensures that a way back to friendship with the Father is made available to every human being.

Closely related to Jesus' Sermon on the Mount is what took place in Exodus 20:1-17. While the Israelites were camping at the foot of Mount Sinai after escaping Egyptian slavery, God spoke to them and covenanted with them. He expressed His love for them, after which He gave them commandments or statutes to equip them to enter into and maintain their relationship with their holy God. The commandments He gave them were an expression of His relational nature and character. Every commandment given to Israel was for the benefit of their relationship with God and each other. They were similar to those that Jesus spoke at the Sermon on the Mount – they were never meant to be harsh legalistic rules.

Scripture teaches us that God is love and that He will never change. This teaches us that when God initiated a relationship with mankind He did so in the context of love. We cannot separate God from love, nor can we separate love from His commandments. They were protocols to assist and enable Old Testament Israel, once liberated from slavery, to walk with God. In today's context, they are meant to guide mankind towards reconciliation with God and thereafter to walk with God.

In order to hear the song of God throughout Scripture, we must see how God's love, His commands and His pursuit of mankind all focus on His intention to be united to the people He loves.

Chapter 2

How God sees it

I n business partnerships, people set up agreements to govern their rights and responsibilities. This means that two equal parties agree to walk together, under rules that govern their relationship and pave the way for mutual benefits. Wisdom teaches these parties to use the services of someone with the necessary expertise in tailoring watertight agreements to facilitate their partnership. This agreement then provides a level of protection that will keep their relationship going, growing and healthy. Steps taken outside the agreement can cause a slowdown, and if not addressed, a permanent breakdown in the relationship. No matter how complete and inclusive the human-made agreement might seem, it cannot fully address every situation that might occur within the business venture.

When we look at the relationship God initiated with Adam after He created him, we see a clear command and a warning about what would either break or benefit the relationship (Genesis 2:9, 16-17). God's command to Adam was both the guideline and boundary of what he was allowed to do to stay in the relationship with God. Scripture is clear – Adam was given a free will and any decision he made would be binding. Whatever he chose to do regarding the two trees in the centre of the garden, would have a direct impact on his relationship with God.

Similarly, when God gave the Ten Commandments to Israel through Moses (Exodus 20:3-17), either obedience or disobedience would have a direct impact on the nation's relationship with God. The ten words of grace, as many call it, were given to the Israelites on two stone tables. The ten words of the commandments embodied God's holy nature. The depth and scope of each word is incredible and extremely powerful. If people truly try to walk in complete adherence to each word, they quickly come to the realisation that it's not possible for any person to constantly comply with God's Ten Commandments. It was never God's intention for His people to walk in holy perfection. Mankind is fallen as a result of Adam's sin, yet, God put forward His holy unchangeable commands. He will not and cannot change who He is and His commandments represent Him on earth. This means that any relationship with God must be built on the platform of these commandments.

Unlike business contracts, which need regular changes made to them, the ten words contained in God's commandments never need changes. They represent God completely in His unchangeable, all-knowing and all-powerful nature. These ten words speak to every tribe, every language and nation, every ethnicity and every culture in the same way. They address humanity as one, because God created them all through our chief ancestor Adam.

Of the ten words, the first four govern our relationship with God, and the last six govern our relationships with the people around us. Jesus did not come to nullify the Ten Commandments given to the Jewish people (Matthew 5:17).

The Ten Commandments were given to the Israelites after their exodus from Egyptian slavery, but Scripture makes it clear that both Jews and Gentiles are part of God's plan (Romans 11:11-31). The Ten Commandments are therefore meant to govern all of humanity (Genesis 49:10).

We have to ask the question: if these commandments are impossible for mankind to fulfil, why were they given to a broken and fallen humanity? I previously mentioned that the Ten Commandments were not given to mankind to allow them to speculate on their successful obedience, the Ten Commandments are a reflection of God's holy nature. The fact that Adam fell through his disobedience did not change who God is. He remains eternally holy. What has changed is how we as humans relate to God's commandments.

When Jesus said in Matthew 5:17 that He came to fulfil the commandments, He meant that by His death on the cross He would become the punishment for disobeying the commandments, while at the same time, all those who believe in Him would become justified before God (2 Corinthians 5:21). This means that when a believer is born again, God bestows the holy nature of Jesus Christ into that person. This does not mean the person has qualified for salvation in any way by their upholding the commandments. It means that Jesus, the sinless suffering servant of God, qualified on our behalf. When God looks at the believer, He sees not our violation of His commandments, He sees Jesus and Him fulfilling the Ten Commandments in their entirety – both in depth and scope.

The way God sees us is the way we are to walk in our relationship with Him. We did not qualify by any of our actions, behaviour or ideology. We qualified to be in a relationship with Him through who Jesus Christ is and us believing in Him. He qualified us by who He is and what He did on our behalf. No wonder the apostle Paul says in Ephesians 2:9 that salvation does not allow any person to boast in their own accomplishments.

We are all the same – we were all condemned by the holy nature of the Ten Commandments. We all were unable to achieve holiness and for this reason God sent His Son to accomplish the fulfilment of the Ten Commandments on our behalf. The way God sees us is not by means of what we can do or achieve. The relationship we have with God requires us to immerse ourselves in Jesus so that His holy nature is reflected in and through us (Romans 5:1and 1 Corinthians 2:16). The apostle Paul said in Galatians 2:20 that he was crucified with Christ and that he no longer lives; Christ now lives in him to completely and exhaustively fulfil all God's requirements of the Ten Commandments in him. His message to us is that we can walk in an intimate relationship with God through the indwelling of Christ. Through this, every requirement regarding every command, from Genesis to Revelation, has been met. We can now celebrate – God in us, with us and for us.

Why Jesus left His heavenly throne

Starting with Genesis and ending in Revelation, Scripture contains several important themes we need to understand. One of these themes is the principle of unity. When opening the Bible, we read how 'God' created the heavens and the earth. Scripture does not detail in the beginning who 'God / the Trinity' is. Only as you progress through Scripture do you begin to see the Triune God being described. A good example is in John 14:16 where Jesus refers to Himself, the Holy Spirit, and the Father as separate persons of the Godhead.

Scripture further reveals how the Godhead talks, reasons and acts in unity when they decide on important matters. Genesis 1:26 uses the term "Let us" which shows how the persons in the Godhead refer to themselves in plurality. The Father, Son and Holy Spirit always agree on everything and by doing so, display and maintain perfect unity.

In Psalm 133:1-3, David says God is drawn to unity among brothers. He says God commands His blessing where there is unity. Where true unity is found, the Spirit of God is allowed to operate in a supernatural manner. We know this because it says God commands His blessing, His life and peace, when brothers dwell in unity. God's blessing means He empowers a person to accomplish what they could not normally do themselves – regardless of their circumstances. His blessing, as David describes it, is everlasting life, which is diametrically opposed to this decaying world. The effects of everlasting life are like Jesus bringing Lazarus back to life after being buried for four days. It is God's authority exercised on earth, despite the prevailing conditions or circumstances.

Scripture says God is love (1 John 4:8). This explains a great deal about God and how His Kingdom is established and operates. Love is the key to fundamental principles such as grace, mercy, kindness, humility and sacrifice. Love is the father of perfect unity. Love also details what God expects of us. Loving God compels me to love my neighbour (Mark 12:31). One cannot divorce our love for God and loving our neighbour. Love speaks unity into existence. The love of God moves me to love Him and in turn causes me to love others. Love is embodied in unity and is expressed by people walking in peace and joy. Unity is not a human invention nor a human faculty. Love and unity are in the same category and together they perfectly express who the Godhead is.

The Trinity and unity

The Trinity created mankind to exist with God in unity forever. Satan sought to destroy this beautiful harmony and set out to force God's hand. He succeeded in tempting and deceiving mankind. Man's fall into sin was the result and God banished mankind from His presence. The effect of sin was so severe that no other creature could solve the problem. Unity between God and His family was lost and had to be restored. God had to personally step in by becoming the sacrifice to re-establish unity between creature and Creator. God's plan of salvation was not just a kind gesture towards humanity. It was the start of a process to fully redeem mankind and restore us back into unity with God.

Having said all that, the question remains: if God saw that it was worthwhile to personally step in and rescue mankind whom He dearly loves, why do we not reciprocate this love? Are we perhaps not seeing how important unity is to God? Is it possible that we have not been taught what true unity is and how it is established? Does Scripture not teach that the reason for the entire salvation plan of God is to ensure eternal unity between Himself and His people?

Unity is the result after the salvation plan of God has come full circle. The finale of unity is what Scripture describes as the marriage supper of the Lamb (Revelation 19:6-9). The apostle John describes what he saw as the new heaven and earth in Revelation 21:1-3. It will be the eternal dwelling of God with His people in unity. This eternal unity between God and His people is what is described as the marriage supper. This banquet is for those who are relationally joined to the bridegroom because a marriage banquet is not for strangers. Jesus Himself made this very clear (Matthew 22:1-7). This eternal banquet is for invited guests who know the bridegroom and whom the bridegroom knows (Matthew 11:11-13).

Proper interpretation of Scripture requires that we look at words used by the authors and interpret their meaning. To make it clear what the author meant when the word 'know' was used in Scripture, we must refer to Genesis 4:1 and see what is said there. This author uses the word 'know', which is correctly interpretated as an intimate relationship and not a platonic friendship. It speaks of the relationship between a husband and wife. The reference is a marital relationship of intimacy, which leads to the conception of children. For a husband and wife to "become one flesh" (Genesis 2:23-25), it cannot take place in the context of a platonic friendship. The word 'know' that Jesus used in Matthew 7:23 is the same usage as in Genesis 4:1. The more we look at this word 'know', the clearer it becomes that God is interested in more than mere friendships with the people He intends to spend eternity with.

Jesus' prayer in John 17 speaks of unity between the Father and Son. In His prayer Jesus mentions that the Trinitarian unity is the foundation and reason for unity between God and people. It sends a clear message that Jesus is the way to the Father (John 17:2). In Jesus' prayer, He says the essence of eternal life is to 'know' the one true God. He speaks of 'knowing' God, which is not meant to describe a brief affiliation (Hebrews 6:4-6). Jesus' words are clearly meant to describe an eternal relationship, not a platonic friendship.

In many instances, preachers, teachers, evangelists, and pastors preach a message of salvation but omit the fact that God not only wants to save His people from their sin, but that the salvation process should lead to a relationship with God. When we read Scripture in an incomplete manner, salvation seems like a mere 'rescue from the fire' event. Jesus did come to earth to ensure redemption for all who believe, but, the Christological event is not all we see in Scripture.

After Jesus died and paid for the sins of the world, the Spirit of God came to permanently indwell the believer. This move, following the death and resurrection of Christ, is God coming down – like the tearing of the temple curtain from top to bottom. It signified making a home with mankind. It does not suggest a cloud hanging over the world. God coming down to earth as the Spirit is what Paul describes as mankind becoming the temple of the Holy Spirit (1 Corinthians 6:19). This indwelling cannot be described as a friendship.

Imagine a parent's child, without them knowing, falls into a river and a stranger risks his own life by jumping into the water and rescuing the child. After the event, the child develops a life-long friendship with the stranger who has become a friend. The friendship developed because of an event that changed the child's life. In salvation terms, a life saved gives rise to great appreciation and a reciprocal life of gratitude on the part of the saved person – or at least this is what is expected.

Many people take what Jesus said about being His friends (John 15:15) and apply it in a way that knowing about God is enough. We must also note what Jesus said in Matthew 7:23 – that knowing Him is more than a distant friendship. Scripture progressively reveals a theme of God with His people, then God for His people, and the finale is God dwelling in His people. Scripture would not describe God indwelling the believer if He only planned to have a distant relationship with us from outer space. If this was the case, the coming of the Holy Spirit was unnecessary.

A single man might consider himself rich and ready for life by himself. When he meets the love of his life and gets married, only then does he begin to truly live a life of fulfilment. The dating and pursuit of the girlfriend who becomes his wife, starts as friendship, and later evolves into a deep relationship. The young man must forsake all others and cling to his wife to become one flesh (Genesis 2:24). The same applies to the relationship between the believer and God. It is worth forsaking all and clinging to God our heavenly Father in the most fulfilling union.

Chapter 3

The golden thread

I 've had the privilege of sitting under the teaching of a few good teachers in both sacred and secular settings. The teachers who, in my view, had the greatest impact on their students and those who helped their students understand and retain the content, were the teachers who connected all the content using a 'golden thread'. This means they used a single theme throughout the work they taught – like a spine connecting all other bones in a body.

In this book, I aim to emulate this principle with God's chief goal for mankind as the golden thread. I trust that every believer who reads this book, will discover that their relationship with God is worth more than anything this world can offer.

The golden thread I see throughout the Bible is that God wants to be with His family. Whether He expresses His family as His wife, or His son, or My people, God is gathering the people He will spend eternity with. Scripture is unequivocal when it portrays God's nature as relational.

1 John 4:8 says that God is love; we know that love cannot exist without the framework of a relationship and vice versa. We also know from Scripture that God's love means He's not a distant and isolated Creator from those He created (John 3:16 and Philippians 2:1-8).

1 Corinthians 6:19 says that God's Spirit has come to dwell in us, which means that God, who is love, now lives in us. Love, being the first attribute ascribed to the Spirit of God, describes the relational nature of God. By having His nature inhabiting us, we are able to build a relationship with Him using what God Himself has deposited in us. Scripture says our bodies are the temple of the Holy Spirit and it is through the Spirit's nature of love and His abiding presence that we are able to respond to God's love. We are able to develop a relationship with God that will ensure we are nurtured, trained, shaped, pruned, corrected, and encouraged. This is the relationship God has in mind and in which we experience love and are loved.

Jesus' teaching in John 10 about the Good Shepherd shows Jesus using the image of a shepherd to teach people about God's love. In John 10:10-12, Jesus says that love has brought life to us (also see Genesis 2:7 and Philippians 2:1-8). Reading John 3:16 (God's love) together with John 10:10 (God's life) makes it clear that God desires us to be relationally connected to Him to experience the fullness of His life and love on earth.

What then about eternity? Well, God is eternal and therefore His love is eternal. Within the body of every believer dwells this eternal wellspring of love that cannot be undone by the death of our earthly bodies.

Throughout the Bible, we see how God has been accomplishing His plan to be relationally connected to His people. Scripture shows how God walked with Israel, His chosen people, in many forms, scenarios and situations. We see God with His people, but not indwelling His people as we see in the New Testament after Jesus' resurrection. Throughout Israel's historical account of the Egyptian exodus, their wanderings through the desert and settling in the Promised Land, Scripture reveals how God walked with His people. He led Israel and fought their wars. As amazing as God's presence was with the Israelites, sin in His people prevented God from indwelling them. The almighty God was limited to manmade structures like tents, tabernacles and temples.

If there was a case to be made regarding true religion, we could compare Christianity, whose God indwells His believers, to other religions whereby their believers seek to find the gods they worship in cold temple buildings. The God of our spiritual father Abraham (Romans 4:12) has shown His desire to be relationally connected to His people. Right from the start in Genesis 2, where God walked with Adam, through to Revelation 21 and 22, we see the purpose of God. Like a golden thread, from creation, throughout history, to today and into eternity, God's eternal plan – residing with His people – is clear.

God's relational ways in Scripture

Scripture helps us to see God's relational ways. Isaiah 41:8 says God was Abraham's friend and Exodus 33:11 speaks of God meeting Moses face-to-face. During this intimate time, God instructed Moses to construct the tabernacle that was to be a meeting place for God and His people (Exodus 19-31). The temporary tabernacle, used during Israel's wanderings in the Wilderness, became a permanent place for God's presence when

Israel lived in the Promised Land. This relational narrative, revealed throughout Scripture, shows us God's eternal plan.

His goal, from the start of creation, was to live with His family – the people He called to be with Him forever. The evidence from Scripture is unmistakable and undeniable. Jesus made this clear to the Samaritan woman at the well in John 4:21. He was foretelling a time when believers of all nations, tribes and tongues – His family – would worship Him in Spirit. This means being with God would not depend on any specific location or in manmade buildings; it means the Spirit of God, indwelling the bodies of every believer, would connect us with God in a way that is closer than a friend, a brother, sister, a father or mother.

As a nation, Israel was like any other nation. However, when God's presence manifested among them, they became a unique people; God selected them to become His "wife" (Isaiah 54:5). Again, in keeping with the golden thread in Scripture, God demonstrates His purpose of cohabiting with His people. Israel, obeying God's commands, was assured of His abiding presence among them. This was made possible by the sacrificial blood of animals, which set them apart as a royal priesthood, a holy nation (Exodus 19:6).

Up to the time of Solomon's grand temple, God dwelt in manmade temples among His people. It took Jesus, the Son of God, to enter a sinful world and become the atoning sacrifice before an everlasting change could take place. After Jesus' death and resurrection, the Spirit of God could permanently indwell His people. John 2:21 says the new temple would be the eternal resurrected body of Jesus, and amazingly, Paul says in 1 Corinthians 12:27 that we are the body of Jesus. Being the body of Christ, also described as the bride of Christ, presents a remarkable future of joyous celebrations as we live with God as His family. Nothing can be compared to a life during which a believer is pursued by a loving God to prepare for an eternal marriage to God. The golden thread connects Genesis 2 to Revelation 19:7, and it helps us see how God fulfils His plan by creating mankind and eventually dwelling with mankind eternally.

When God's eternal goal becomes clear, which is to be with His people, we begin to understand the big picture Scripture is painting. We no longer get bogged down in our spiritual growth by focusing on single goals such as the birth and the cross of Christ, Pentecost, sanctification and the church. We begin to understand these important items as part of the greater purpose of God.

The crown of His creation

When God created man on the sixth day of creation, He formed man and enabled him to relate to his Creator. To relate means to have the ability to form a friendship. How does this take place? Mankind was given a unique position above all other creatures on earth, and still holds this position today. Not only was mankind created in the image and likeness of God, but they were also infused with the Spirit, the breath of God. This indwelling of God's Spirit is what makes it possible for a person to be God's friend – it means we can understand God's commands and we have the ability to obey or disobey them (see Genesis 2:15-20).

The apostle Paul states in 2 Corinthians 13:14 that the love of the Father is expressed in us by means of His fellowshipping Spirit. This is the way we are helped to understand the person of God. Paul also says in 1 Corinthians 2:1-16 that in order for us to understand God, we need His Spirit to indwell us; no other being in heaven or on earth has been given this privilege. Peter says even angels long to understand this (see 1 Peter 1:12^b). To the Old Testament Israelites, it meant that God Himself dwelt among them (Exodus 29:45-46), but to us, the New Israel of God, comprising all believers, God indwells us (John 17:22-23 and Galatians 4:6). There's a big difference.

Mankind's position before God is far higher than that of the animals. Yet, because of mankind's fallen state, they began worshipping objects lesser than themselves – meaning images in the animal kingdom (Romans 1:22). God does not commune with the animals in the same way He does with mankind. In fact, Scripture says God feeds the animals daily and has provided them with everything they need. Scripture shows that God has a very special relationship with mankind.

Genesis 1:27-28 says God created mankind in His image and likeness and then blessed them. This blessing was not extended to any other created beings, which means it is not for animals that Jesus was incarnated to come to earth and die. Jesus left the glory of His Father's side to atone for mankind's sin. He was the mediator of the New Covenant, in His own blood, so mankind could be restored back to friendship with God. The relationship we have with God is unique and requires careful understanding in order to enter and maintain it. Mankind was and still is the crown of God's creation. What this means is that mankind was created for a special purpose, which is to have a meaningful relationship with God.

The principle of relationships was not created when mankind was created. It has always been part of the essence of the Godhead. Part of the outflow of the relationship within the Godhead was the establishment of a relationship between a man and a woman, which is expressed in the covenant of marriage. God's intention for marriage was that it should embody a deep companionship or friendship, reflecting the kind of relationship God intended to have with mankind (Ephesians 5:31-32). The principle of relationships is one of the most precious things God has given mankind.

As with everything else God created, Satan entered the stage and set out to either distort or destroy everything God created. His main focus, from the beginning, was the relationships God instituted. For example, Satan's distortion of love has caused mankind to grapple with the different kinds of love. We as humans have been created to show and receive love – we desire to show *agape* love, but fall into *eros* love, which is more of a selfish desire and is based on the lust of the eyes. Because of this distortion, *eros* love ignores the needs of the other party. Similarly, people have turned away from their place of authority and became absorbed with each other. God's powerful institution of relationships has become the main target of the devil. Satan's main aim is to destroy man's relationship with God and with each other, which is the most precious thing God can give any created being.

From the first days of creation, God was in the process of building a dwelling place He could occupy with those who belong to Him and want to be with Him. Despite Satan's best attempts to separate mankind from God, God is fulfilling this goal. From eternity-to-eternity God always was, is, and will always be a relational Being. Everything God does is from this perspective. Solomon, the wisest man ever, says that all things accomplished under the sun are empty, meaningless and vain – if done without God. Solomon concludes in Ecclesiastes 12:13 that people were created to have a relationship with their Maker while they have the breath to do so.

The kiss of life

Scripture teaches us that God is omniscient. But just how up close and personal is God to His creation? Scripture also teaches us that we were created in God's own image and likeness and that He placed an insatiable desire in us to be close to Him. It was never God's intention to be a stranger. He created mankind with a built-in intentional dependence on our Creator. This dependence is expressed as part of the relationship between God and man. God demonstrated His desired closeness to us by breathing the breath of life into mankind at creation.

God did not perform the same intimate procedure on any other created beings, such as birds or animals, and because of this uniqueness, we have a close relationship with God. As the Trinity, God linked Himself inextricably and forever to mankind through the New Covenant in the blood of His Son Jesus Christ. This link is more than a promise – it is an oath in God's own incarnated blood. It is truly a mystery to us that God would link Himself in such a deep way to mankind. It is not surprising that the author of Hebrews asks why God is mindful of mankind.

Not only did God give mankind the kiss of life, He shed His blood for us to reconcile us to Himself. Those who are reconciled, Scripture says, are now *in Christ*. This is an important theme, especially in the New Testament writings of Paul. Being *in Christ* is a position no other created being can ever experience. God has forged a relationship with mankind, described in John 14:16, which starts with His plan of salvation through the cross of Christ and it continues by way of the Spirit of God, the Helper, being with man forever.

Genesis 2:7 says: "God breathed the breath of life into man's nostrils." Have you ever felt someone in a queue bumping into you? Does it not feel strange when someone you don't know unexpectedly touches you? Does it not feel invasive? But when loved ones touch each other it does not seem strange and uncomfortable.

Now that we understand God's intention to have an intimate relationship with those who respond to His call, we can begin to develop a relationship with God and we can do the same with our children. The earlier that parents introduce their children to God, the deeper their relationship with God will grow.

In Exodus, we see how God met with Israel at Mount Sinai immediately after their escape from slavery. God met with them and remained with them on their journey into the Promised Land. His intentions back then are still the same today – to be with the people who respond to His love. The kiss of life begins our journey with God, but it is our responsibility to be mindful of what develops a sustained friendship with God and what could impede this friendship.

Part Two

Why is it important?

Chapter 4

In Jesus' own words

Our lives are spent working as we run from one task to another, and at various stages of our lives, we are occupied with many activities. Some tasks are voluntary and some are part of our daily workplace responsibilities. From youth to adulthood, we occupy ourselves with the responsibilities related to raising children and their schedules. After this we busy ourselves with midlife activities, and before we know it, our effective years have passed in front of our eyes. It is at this point that we realise time is something we can never recover.

When Jesus was teaching a crowd regarding warnings and encouragements (Luke 12-13), a question was put to Him by someone in the crowd: "Teacher, tell my brother to divide the inheritance with me." Interestingly, Jesus responded to the question, knowing that others would benefit from the answer. He warned people about choosing sides without knowing the facts, then He followed with a stunning rebuke. In this Lukan passage, chapter 12:13-21, Jesus highlighted the problem regarding greed, using the parable of a rich fool. He spoke about people's efforts spent gathering worldly possessions and the way these possessions give birth to man's insatiable desire for more.

Mentioning worldly possessions, Jesus hinted at people's busyness, which is associated with wealth. What Jesus said in verse 15 summed up man's destiny: "Life does not consist in an abundance of possessions" (cross reference 1 Timothy 6:9). Jesus made the point that life on earth has a deeper meaning than the worthless gathering of earthly possessions. Solomon's own conclusion in Ecclesiastes 2 was similar. He concluded that the accumulation of great wealth was utterly meaningless.

While teaching the crowd in Luke 12, Jesus pointed out the limited years mankind has on earth and the authority God has over all creation. He then made the connection between man's limited time on earth, the futility of gathering worldly wealth, and the need for people to make an all-out effort to become "rich towards God". This Scripture has stayed with me for many years, and developed in me a burning question: what does it mean to be rich towards God? Obviously, Jesus has already ruled out worldly possessions, He has spoken against legalism, and has also rejected religious observation of the Mosaic Law (Romans 4:13). Jesus made it clear that merely studying Scripture will not fulfil what it takes to be rich towards God (John 5:39-40). When we look at what Jesus cites in the Lukan parable, we get a glimpse of what riches to God could mean. If Jesus warns us against spending great effort collecting things which rust, corrode and get stolen (Matthew 6:19-20), then to be rich towards God means we have to collect what is everlasting. The next question is: what can we invest in that is everlasting?

In this passage in Luke, we hear Jesus echo the words of Solomon in Ecclesiastes. Solomon made the statement that whatever is done without God is worthless. Making thirty similar statements to "Vanity, vanity" and "All things that are done under the sun ... all is vanity." Solomon wanted to tell all people that amassing worldly wealth is futile. He did so by studying his own pursuits and those of mankind, which led him to the conclusion that mankind can only be fulfilled when we truly know God our Maker (Ecclesiastes 12:13).

Solomon came to the conclusion that mankind is asking the wrong question. It is not important what mankind seeks to reach fulfilment; it is what God seeks, and mankind's pursuit of that, that brings true fulfilment. The sovereign God created mankind for the purpose of fellowship. No other created object can ever fill the gap that was left when man fell into sin and lost the friendship of God (Genesis 3:10). When Jesus referred to "life" and "possessions" in Luke 12:15, He made it clear that God is relational and that possessions cannot fulfil the need in mankind to relate to God. Humanity was created with a hunger to have relations with each other and with God – this is the core of what Jesus meant when He said to be "rich towards God" in Luke 12:21[b].

When life ends on earth for every human being, the only thing we can take with us, which is worth more than all our possessions, and the only thing that God is interested in, is the relationship we built with Him in our allotted time on earth. Relationships are the most valuable possession we have been given by God Himself.

Relationships are like bridges between people and between us and God, which allow love, compassion, healing, and many other valuable intangible gifts to be exchanged. Relationships express the heart of God, as was displayed in the salvation gift of God's

Son to a broken world. God gave the Son He loves to rescue the other sons and daughters He loves. What God expressed on the cross was a clear sign of what He values most, which is restored relationships.

A young man, mentioned in Mark 10:22, walked away from the Saviour of the world, saddened by the fact that Jesus gave him an ultimatum. The passage in Mark 10 speaks of a leader who had amassed great wealth, and who chose to pursue worldly possessions rather than a relationship with Jesus. This man relinquished his eternal inheritance, his eternal reward, for earthly possessions, temporary feel-good items he could own. The Spirit of God chose to include this man's folly in Scripture so we can learn from it. The man's wealth had grown roots in his heart; not only was his heart set on his wealth, but also on his identity, his emotions and his self-styled status.

Before anyone can turn their back on worldly wealth and pursue a relationship with God, that person must have their heart and mind illuminated by the Spirit of God. If this was a "quick and easy fix", then the rich young ruler in Mark 10 would have walked away from His wealth and followed Jesus immediately. If he recognised what true riches in God are, he would have abandoned his worldly pursuits. Sadly, he could not fathom such a move. Only the Spirit of God, the Spirit of fellowship between God and mankind, can illuminate the hearts and minds of people to see beyond the temporary deceitful riches this world offers. In Jesus' own words in John 3:6: "Flesh gives birth to flesh, but the Spirit (upper case) gives birth to spirit." Let Scripture speak for itself when it says we are to walk by the Spirit (again upper case) so that we do not give in to the cravings of the flesh. It says the Spirit is at war with the flesh (Galatians 5:16-17), which means the young ruler walked away from Jesus. He chose to pursue the fleshly desires raging in him and not the Spirit's voice. He chose the pursuit of wealth over fellowship with God, which was Jesus' actual warning in Luke 12:21.

Considering Jesus' advice to be rich toward God instead of pursuing worldly wealth, we need to establish how we become rich towards God. A good way to start is to go to the Old Testament and see what God said about His relationship with His people Israel. From these encounters, we can draw some conclusions as far as what pleased God and what displeased Him. His walk with Israel was described by God as the relationship between a husband and a wife (Jeremiah 31:32). In many cases, God's walk with Israel was similar to how God walked with Adam in the Garden. God set out to dwell with Israel and His presence was constantly with them. God did whatever was necessary to deal with Israel's sin in order to be with His people.

In the New Testament we see what Paul wrote in Ephesians 5:21-33 about the conduct of a husband and wife. He said this relationship is a picture of Christ and His bride. When we desire to know what it means to be rich toward God, we cannot be given a more descriptive example than a marital relationship from God's perspective. Two key issues in any relationship are those of love and trust, enacted by a total abandonment of self. It is selfless service to the other partner. This is what God is looking for. When people find this kind of relationship, they agree that it is worth abandoning all the riches of this world to pursue true love. This is to become rich toward God.

Chapter 5

Overturning the misnomer

Have you ever asked yourself why we have to work every day? We all have to put in a day's labour, because this is what Scripture commands in Genesis 3:17-19. I have looked at this from many different angles and I'm convinced that there is more to life than working.

After mankind sinned, was their greatest loss the punishment of daily toil, or was it the loss of fellowship with their Creator? When we look at how people spend their days, we have to ask the question, could our frustrations and excessive work ethic be signs of a failed attempt to achieve or re-establish a friendship with God? When Jesus died on the cross as the pinnacle of God's plan of salvation, was it to restore man's energy to work or to restore man back into fellowship with God?

Let's see what Scripture reveals. For millennia people have tried to attain salvation by leading good or moral lives and doing good deeds, through which they hope to receive a pardon from God for their sins. They live lives that, from the outside, seem exemplary, yet they have within them a burning uncertainty about how many good works will qualify them for eternal life. This is the same question raging within Jewish and Muslin believers. This work ethic has driven people to achieve bigger and greater feats of engineering and scientific development, and people are working themselves to a standstill to try to reach a place where they can say they solved their own problems. This is reflected in the Scriptural passage about salvation by grace through faith. When Paul says in Ephesians 2:8 that faith is a gift, he excludes any efforts on a person's part to achieve good standing before God.

When we realise that we live by God's gift of grace and faith, we rest from our attempts to please God to achieve His favour (Hebrews 4:3). We learn in Exodus 33:14 that there will be no rest without the presence of God. The rest Scripture refers to is the people of God walking with Him in the way they were created to; without pressure to do things to receive God's acceptance. This is where fellowship, unity, love and companionship are found.

These are made possible only when the hindrance of sin has been removed by the process of salvation by grace through faith (Ephesians 2:8-9). What is important here is that salvation is received as a gift of God, not through people's works. For as long as people busy themselves with work, they cannot enter the rest of and fellowship with God.

Does being at 'rest' mean passive or active rest? Were people created to work only, or to fellowship with God and work? In Genesis 2:15, Scripture says God "put" man in the Garden of Eden to work it and take care of it. Looking deeper, we find this verse actually describes what it means to be in God's presence. We read how Adam walked with God in the Garden of Eden – before man fell into sin. Placing man in the Garden of Eden meant he was at rest in God's presence, while he had to work the Garden. Yet, he did not have to do anything to win God's favour. He had to tend to the Garden and walk with God in order to remain in God's rest and to experience inner peace. The Hebrew term for what God did with Adam after creating him, was to 'rest' him in the Garden of Eden. This suggests man was placed in the Garden to be with God and not 'put' in the Garden merely to work it (Genesis 2:15).

In modern English translations, 'put' unfortunately omits a deep-seated and profound Hebrew context, depicting worship. This use of the word signifies the placement of something in the presence of the Lord for the purpose of worship (reference: Exodus 16:33-34, Leviticus 16:23; Numbers 17:4; Deuteronomy 26:4, 10). The correct interpretation of the action of God in Genesis 2:15 was to place man in the sanctuary of the Garden where he could rest and be safe, and where man was 'put' into the garden in God's presence where he could have fellowship with God. In a more literal translation: God 'rested' man in the garden to worship before Him and obey His command. We can conclude then that man's purpose was to be in God's presence in the Garden or Sanctuary of God for fellowship and worship, and not only to work it and take care of the Garden.

The misnomer that needs to be corrected is that man must always be working in order to please God. Hebrews 11:6 makes it clear that if believers want to please God, they are to walk by faith, which is not a process by which we win God's favour by our achievements. Rather, faith is trusting God for all we need. This trust can be expressed as being in God's presence and obediently following His commands. Our focus should be less on doing things for God and more on walking closely with Him (Luke 10:42).

Chapter 6

Looking into God's world

During my daily tasks I interact with people, and in these times, I often ask myself this question: what is a day like in God's world? What does He choose as His favourite activity, or where does He like to spend His time? What demanding activities fill His day and what kinds of events get His attention? We only need to turn to Genesis 2 to find that God has an affinity for fellowship with those He created. We see that God chose to take time to walk with Adam in the Garden. He set aside time in His day to dialogue with the man He created.

From Genesis we jump all the way to Ephesians. Instead of seeing how God spends time with one person, we see what is on God's mind and how He likes to order His world. In Ephesians 2:16 we see that God's desire is to have all men, regardless of their colour, nationality, or culture, be reconciled to each other and to Him. God does not seek the presence of hostility and He will take extreme measures to deal with separation. He did so when Adam sinned in Genesis 3 and He's doing the same in Ephesians 2.

God's world is a domain where relationships exist in a state of reconciliation. Ephesians 2:14 says God went to extremes to achieve His goal – a reconciled world. God's goal, His focus and aim could only be achieved if He involved Himself, and He was willing to suffer and die to achieve peace between humanity and Himself.

I believe Ephesians can be described as: 'The way God's world works.' I say this because no other book in the Bible gives us such an in-depth look into God's relational world. In Ephesians 2 Paul says God's world will be a world without sin (death and separation), which is the enemy of any relationship (Ephesians 4:18). Also in Ephesians 2, Paul says God projects what the future will be by reconciling mankind to Himself and to each other through the man Jesus Christ. God's world will see one body, one people under God (Ephesians 3:6).

Ephesians 5 tells us how we are to live and treat each other in God's world while here on earth. We are not to pollute the household of God with darkness. Ephesians 5:23-33 tells us God has established an unbreakable bond between Himself and His church, which He calls His bride. It is a bond not even death can sever, and is described by Paul as "a profound mystery" (Ephesians 5:32). Our minds struggle to conceive how God can invite us into a bond of holy matrimony with Him forever.

To help us understand His world, God gives us Scriptural guidelines and time here on earth to practice what His world, where we eternally abide with Him, will be like. Ephesians 3:14 connects heaven and believers here on earth by calling us one family. God is on track to create one family for Himself. The glory of God in heaven is embodied in the church on earth through Christ, its head, and the members of this heavenly household on earth will be known by their love for each other (Ephesians 4:2,16). In God's world there is only one Lord, one body, one Spirit, one hope, one faith, and one Father God over all (Ephesians 4:4-6).

The Bible says, "God is love", and it also tells us that whoever wants to live in God's world must follow the way of God's world, which is love (1 John 4:7). God expressed His love when He began the process of repairing our broken world that He created as perfect before sin entered. Before man was excommunicated by God after his sin, God promised a plan of salvation (Genesis 3:15). The full outworking of God's plan of reconciliation sees a new world, resembling a place of total harmony, peace and love. This is the place God intended from the beginning. It is His world where things operate His way, people abide by His truth and all remain in His love. In order for God to achieve His world, our broken world has to be transformed. We see this portrayed in Revelation 22.

How does God want the world to perceive Him? Apart from making His invisible attributes, His eternal power and divine nature, visible to mankind through what He created, God has chosen the relationship between Himself and the church to be the very aspect that explains to the world who He is. Ephesians 3:10 says the church, the bride of Christ, is God's way of making His wisdom known to the world. He has not chosen any other way but this example of a beautiful intimate relationship between two very unequal parties. The Creator has chosen to take in a prodigal, a vagrant wife, a disobedient family, a people who have deserted a close Friend, and has used the process of reconciliation as a demonstration of His love, mercy and grace to the world.

Truth at the heart of reconciliation

In doing this, He has communicated truth, which is at the heart of His plan of reconciliation. In God's world, truth is at the centre. His world does not contain falsehood or uncertainty. When we are drawn into His world through reconciliation, we are drawn into a domain where truth prevails, rules and governs. It is for this reason that Paul says the nature of the Kingdom of God begins with righteousness (Romans 15:17).

God does not have a worldview. He is the view the world has to adopt. He is the source of life, provision and protection. In God's world, He is at the centre. Anything contrary will resemble the rebellious act of the Tower of Babel in Genesis 11. While God is communicating reconciliation, He is also communicating truth to a world that wants to establish its own 'truth'. In God's world, truth governs, sustains and protects. If we want to live, operate and remain in His world, we need to adopt truth. In God's world, truth has existed before creation. Truth was not created; it existed within God as His nature. The moment truth is distorted, relationships suffer. In God's world, truth heals relationships. It sets people free from whatever causes separation between parties and it keeps them relating to each other and God.

Living on an island

One of the biggest reasons for this book is to highlight how we live today. Not all Christians, after being saved, live a life that resembles what Scripture requires of them. Despite God providing all we need for life and godliness, many Christians live as if they are bordering on burnout or defeat. Something is missing.

Throughout Scripture, the presence of God has sustained God's people. The fountainhead every believer needs to find is with God. In His presence, life abounds, wisdom dwells, victory is in His hand, and His eternal Kingdom is at hand. If a statistical analysis were to be done, we would find that most Christians would lack a key aspect seen in Scripture. Because modern Christians lack the presence of God, although they see the odd supernatural event take place, they still live in a very self-sustaining way, and little of God's wisdom is seen in their actions.

It would appear as if Christians were rescued, during their salvation-event, and afterwards placed on an island. They begin to live in a new way, yet this new way is not sustained.

When a believer lives on an island, they develop ways to become self-sufficient. Their entire mindset is to decide for themselves; to control their own actions; they submit to no one else but themselves, and they work to secure their own future. This island existence stops the believer from becoming truly and utterly dependent on God. When such a person remains isolated from God, although they are born again in the spirit, they are unable to cry out to God for help. Their hearts might have been illuminated by the life of God, but their lives remain in darkness.

An island existence bars the believer from walking with God daily. It keeps the reborn person at a level of spirituality where they are unable to achieve anything significant. It is as if the enemy could not prevent the person from being born again, but he is now succeeding in keeping the newborn believer from living a supernatural life of victory and wisdom. The believer on the island is convinced that they are living the ultimate life. They assume that this is God's best for them – His ultimate goal. Unfortunately, the island life is a life of ignorance and weakness. It was never God's intention to see a newborn baby deported to an island where they are removed from enjoying fellowship with Him and benefiting from His divine life and love. The island existence has no relevance nor reference to eternal life with God. What God has planned for every believer is to live with Him in a divine relationship eternally. The process that will see every believer achieve this union with God, starts while we live on earth. It is during our daily walk that we learn to be with God and He with us. Life as we know it, is God's plan for us to get to know Him better and to develop our relationship with Him.

What a relationship unlocks

Mankind manufactures, acquires and stores things they regard as valuable. Throughout the ages, these finite things have been deemed valuable by mankind. Can we find, create, or develop an infinite resource or commodity that unlocks something bigger than ourselves? No, our only hope is to link up with something or someone greater than ourselves, and in order to build a relationship with such an entity or being, we have to find a person to relate to. This is the very resource, namely our relationship with the Creator of the universe, that can unlock mankind's existence on earth and beyond. Our ultimate pursuit should be a relationship beyond the physical aspects and attributes of our own wisdom and this finite planet. God created people with the ability to respond to Him on a spiritual level, and this has been God's desire since the days of creation – establishing a meaningful relationship between God and man.

Based on that, I want to highlight key aspects from Scripture. It is the narrative of God's family; mankind as God created us. As Creator, God demonstrated His love towards the people He created. When we read Scripture and we miss this crucial aspect of God's family, we ignore what God the Father desires. Scripture is clear that God seeks to be with His family, the people who love Him and wilfully obey Him. God is a relational God and has expressed this fact throughout the whole of Scripture. He protects, provides and nourishes His family within the relational bond He has established. It is within this bond, the boundaries around 'family', where God releases His promises. I want to briefly touch on a few aspects that relationships can unlock, and that impact our lives daily.

The first aspect is within the family and is the power of a father's love for his children. The second is the authority a father exercises over his children. The third is revelation knowledge available to those who walk with God. The last aspect is God's way of relational partnership.

The power of a father's love

The bond of a father and his children is unlike any other. A true father will go to great lengths to locate and return his children if they have been removed from him against his will.

What would God the Father do, should someone drive a wedge between Him and His family? Can you and I imagine the deep anguish of a father whose children have been taken away from him? To any parent, this is a time of severe anxiety and concern until they are reunited with their child. Until the child is found, the parent will not sleep, eat or stop looking for the missing child. Many parents who, due to difficult circumstances, gave up children for adoption, carry a deep desire to be reunited with their children.

In John 5, we read Jesus' statements in an encounter with several Jewish leaders. Jesus was clear that He came to seek and save the lost. But who are the lost? The lost are all of humanity who have been separated from God through sin. In verse 17, Jesus said that He and His Father are constantly at work to restore God's children back to Him. If His children were all with Him, He would not have any reason for working. Scripture details how God had a plan, before the creation of the world, to ensure His children are returned to Him. He will not rest until His family is reunited and the evil one, who deceitfully removed them from Him, is punished. God's plan to re-establish relations with His family extends beyond our understanding. God Himself gave of Himself to restore His own back to Him. This is what the power of 'family' has made God do, and it is for this reason that the evil one will not rest until he has destroyed the institution of marriage.

The authority a father imparts to his children

The authority God chooses to pass onto others only takes place within the boundaries of the relationships He has established. God called and empowered Moses to lead His people. He showed Himself to Moses (Exodus 33:12-23). In stark contrast to Saul, Israel's first king from whom God withdrew, Moses was a friend of God and operated with great power from God. Seen within the relationships between parents and children; governments and citizens; leadership and the church body, and so on, God has established and uses relationships when partnering with mankind in His Kingdom.

Jesus was clearly impressed by a centurion in Matthew 8:5-13 who understood God's chain of command. This man understood that authority cannot be usurped or be self-appointed. Today we attach love and romance to our understanding of relationships, but this centurion correctly understood that authority, up and down the structures, can only exist within the boundaries of a relationship. His explanation helps us understand that authority is God's to give to those who are in a relational bond with Him. The understanding he exemplified, which Jesus called faith, unlocked power from heaven to achieve what was possible for God and impossible for humans.

A key reason why we should value what God values is because we need to value relationships as much as He does. In order to achieve what is of value, we have to be in a relationship with the one who has given the command, and the necessary command structures are found within a relationship.

We see this clearly when we read John 5:16-30. Here Jesus addresses a group of religious leaders who have usurped power over people based on their knowledge of the Law. They use traditions and practices, shaped into laws, to govern and oppress people. The religious leaders mentioned in John 5 operated in a pseudo authority, yet had no relational structure in which God's authority filtered down to and through them. We see this when Jesus speaks of "My Father" and not "your Father". He accuses them of being self-styled leaders who have no authority. Jesus makes it clear that His authority comes from His relationship with His Father. Through this relationship He has received the power to have and give eternal life, to judge, to receive honour and to condemn. All these are eternal powers, which can only be transferred to someone else where love, obedience, trust and unity exist. The authority of God has been handed down the relational structure of Father to Son as we see in John 5:39-40. The Father has passed on all His authority to Jesus His Son, who in turn passes authority onto those who He knows and who know Him.

It is no surprise that Jesus says, "Apart from Me you can do nothing" (John 15:5). He fully understood that His power and authority stem from His relationship with His Father. His words and works have been given to Him (John 5:19). If this applies to Jesus, how much more should we be pursuing this kind of relationship? Jesus was referring to achievements that hold eternal value, not the kind of possessions that evaporate, get stolen or rust, nor knowledge that ages into obsoleteness (Matthew 6:19-21). The resource God wants us to pursue is a relationship with Him which will unlock eternal value, unending possession, lasting joy, and fulfilment.

The relationship between a father and his children is a platform for the deepest trust to be built and maintained. The greater the trust, the greater the authority that can be transferred. In the same way, forgiveness and repentance can be given and received using this platform. A father's approval of his children unlocks their future potential and gives them freedom to operate in their father's name; it allows for vulnerability when corrected, and it opens the door for transferring gifts, skills, and values from the father to the child. This relationship is truly a resource worth pursuing.

Revelation from God

The closer you are to a person, the better you get to know them. As Christians, our walk with God should be a dialogue, communicating with Him in prayer. Having His Spirit, yielding to His voice, and studying His Word, allows Him to communicate with us. God's Word is our instruction manual regarding everything God wants to communicate with us, including the origin of the universe and mankind. His Word informs us regarding our conduct, about sin, evil and the war between God and the devil.

God's Word teaches us all we need to know for life and godliness. It gives us structure in life by giving us the boundaries we are to live in. By studying Scripture, we know who we are, who God is, what our purpose in life is, what God expects from us, and how we can relate to Him. Through the partnership between God's Word and the Spirit illuminating our minds to understand the Word, we receive revelation. Revelation is what we get from the Spirit of God about what His Word contains; it's knowledge that God reveals to us about Himself and everyday life.

The important principle is that those who choose to walk close to God will receive more revelation than those who don't. Walking with God in a friendship requires setting aside other distractions. These are people who 'buy out the time' to devote themselves to God.

The closer we walk with God, the deeper trust develops and opens the door to revelation from God. A link exists between our relationship with God and the revelation we get from it. I would like to highlight this link by introducing a new word, 'Revelation-ship'. Jesus Himself highlighted this in John 14:21. He said that the person who has His commandments and who keeps them demonstrates their love for God, which is a direct expression of a relationship with God. Jesus then said this relationship will allow reciprocal love, which in turn, will allow Jesus to reveal more of Himself to the person. The relationship the believer has with God unlocks revelation, which empowers the believer and deepens the love.

Chapter 7

God's relational partnership

God is sovereign. He possesses supreme and ultimate power. He is self-sufficient and can do whatever, wherever and however He wants. He does not need council from anyone apart from within the Trinity. God can make plans and see to it that they are fulfilled. He is not threatened by anything or anyone. The phrase, "God's sovereignty and human responsibility" teaches us that God can decide and act by Himself. At the same time, God gives mankind the choice to obey or disobey and decide his own destiny. God will never force a person to do anything, and by choosing to follow the Spirit's lead, we walk in God's will and His ways.

That said, it remains a mystery why God chooses to partner with us. Through the salvation He provides, God calls mankind to believe in Him, to be His adopted children, and to be co-labourers and co-heirs with His Son Jesus Christ. He calls us to partner with Him in bringing others into His plan of eternal life. Words cannot describe what God has made available to a world that has largely walked away from His friendship. In Ephesians 5:32-33, Paul describes what God has done as a "mystery". God sent His Son to save His people from their sin. When Jesus had completed His salvation mission, He founded the church and commissioned His disciples to continue His salvation mission. The arrival of the Spirit of God empowered humans to do the work God has called them to do (Acts 1:8). Although God is sovereign and can execute His own plans, He calls men to partner with Him to share the Good News of His salvation plan with others. Despite man's brokenness, God partners with mankind to accomplish His will. It's like a fit athlete choosing to run a race with his own young children. They will slow him down drastically, but his grace will allow them all to finish the race together so they all can celebrate afterwards.

This partnership God calls us into is a friendship based on love and trust (1 John 3:1). God as the benefactor calls us to partner with Him and provides all we need to accomplish the task He has given us. God's love, grace, mercy, wisdom, anointing, power, and authority are all available to us to fulfil the salvation mission we have been called to.

The process God followed with Israel

Why is Old Testament Israel such an important source of knowledge for us today? The Old Testament reveals the intentional relationship God built with His people and how it was constituted. This takes us back to Genesis 1 and 2 where God created mankind to live with Him.

The process God followed with Israel is in Scripture for us to learn from. In the books of Exodus, Leviticus, Numbers and Deuteronomy, we see three sequential steps that make up the process God followed to fully reconcile Israel to Himself – the sheep of His pasture. It's important to note that it was three completed steps. When seen together, these three steps form the pillars of God's plan to free His people and to develop them, in order to co-habit with them. God's goal, demonstrated in the lives of the Old Testament Israel, was to live with His people, in His land, under His rule.

The Pillar of Freedom

God started with what we call the exodus from Egypt. It's important to see that everything is done through the revealed power of God. This step incorporated the ten plagues and the blood of a lamb on the doorposts of every Jewish household. They were to wait inside their houses, behind the blood, applying their faith and trusting God's Word. The angel of judgement then struck down every firstborn in every house in Egypt where no blood was applied. This process, leaving slavery by the blood of the lamb, is called the Pillar of Freedom from Slavery. To us it is the New Testament (Ephesians 2:8-10) picture of justification by grace through faith – the freedom from sin. From here they walked through the Sea of Reeds on dry land, symbolising water baptism – still part of the Pillar of Freedom from Slavery.

Pillar of the Wilderness

Next, God embarked on a nation-building plan. He had Israel camp at Mount Sinai where He appeared to every person from the top of the mountain. He gave them the Ten Commandments though Moses and covenanted with the whole nation. He spoke to them and all of Israel agreed.

This step is receiving God's transforming Word and experiencing His power and closeness. This step is similar to Jesus' Sermon on the Mount (Matthew 5-7). God appeared to them in power as a symbol, similar to the Holy Spirit event in Acts 2. The transforming Word of God they received on two stone tablets were what the Holy Spirit would use to wash and transform them as they journeyed for forty years in the Wilderness.

In New Testament terms this part is seen as the believer's sanctification. Through the Spirit applying the Word of God, He washes away old mindsets and beliefs. He also questions wrong practices and traditions. It's a place of hearing the Word, making mistakes, getting up, hearing the Word, and repeating the process until we choose to do what's correct. Amazingly, God empowers us as believers by His Spirit as we are born, learn to crawl, and then walk. Patience is required as God repeatedly trains us to understand right from wrong (Hebrews 5:14). During this time of 'growing up', God is a constant gracious companion.

This part of the process, the Sinai Desert journey, is called the Wilderness pillar. The commandments God gave His people were an exact reflection of His Person and Nature. The laws were meant to instruct Israel how to behave within their relationship with God in a way that they honour God's holiness. We see in Isaiah 54:5 and Hosea 2:19 that God saw Israel as His covenant wife – the covenant of marriage is the deepest and most profound expression of a relationship there is (Ephesians 5:22-33).

Pillar of the Promised Land

The final part of the journey God took Israel on was the crossing of the River Jordan into Canaan – the Promised Land. This stage of the journey came after Israel was justified (freed from sin slavery) and had been sanctified (trained in the Wilderness Walk). Their final goal was to establish themselves, to pioneer cities and towns, and to engage in warfare. They had to drive out the pagan nations occupying the land in order to take possession of what God promised Abraham in Genesis 12:1-3. It would be the glory days of Israel as the promises of God made to Abraham were fulfilled – a time of joyful celebration, and of peace and prosperity. This is the last of the three pillars and it is called the Pillar of the Promised Land. We see this pillar to be the glorification of the people of God. In New Testament terms it resembles the final two chapters in Revelation where God resides with His people in the eternal city; in His land and under His rule.

To recap, the three-part journey above known as Egypt-Wilderness-Promised Land require that all parts be completed (1 Corinthians 1:30). Together the parts symbolise the believer's completed process of salvation. Freedom from slavery was never God's only goal. It was merely His first step. We are to grow and develop until we reach maturity where we establish the Kingdom of God in our lives and in everything around us.

The three pillars of salvation detail how God built a relationship with His people, Old Testament Israel. Jesus mentions a similar theme in John 14:2, saying He is going to prepare a place for every believer in His Father's house. This is a clear indication of what God has in store for His people; His intentions have not changed since Genesis 2.

In the New Testament Paul addresses breakdowns within the Corinthian church's relational unity. He connects Old Testament Israel's journey to that of the New Testament church. Paul uses Israel's history to warn the Corinthian believers not to fall away from God because of temptation (1 Corinthians 10:1-13). So many of God's people in the Wilderness and the Promised Land did not persevere in their relationship with God. Similar to Adam and Eve, because of temptation, many Israelites fell out of their relationship with God and were separated from God. Paul's account of the Israelites' journey shows how they dishonoured their relationship with God by entertaining 'extra-marital affairs' with the gods of other nations. In verse 11, Paul says that the account of Israel is written down as an example to warn us not to neglect our relationship with God.

The three steps of Egypt, Wilderness and Promised Land should be understood and used as mutually independent; they are separate sequential events, but together they form part of the completed pattern God set out for Old Testament Israel. If one step is elevated over the collective value of the three steps, believers will not achieve the full extent of what God has in store for them. It will prevent them experiencing the fullness of the relationship God had intended since creation.

Every relationship is founded on the principle of mutual expectations. As believers we are quick to express our needs to God, which are the expectations we have. We often don't pay attention to the expectation God has of us. This is mainly because we are not taught the meaning of the full pattern – the completed three steps of Egypt, Wilderness and Promised Land. Leaving one or two steps out mean that believers are not able to mature in their relationship with God.

Say for instance, they only know the escape from Egypt, meaning the day they were declared righteous by grace through faith, they will not be able to enjoy the fullness of God's promises. This step must be followed by the Wilderness Walk of development and finally, by entering God's rest, when the believer is in the Promised

Land, enjoying God's peace, prosperity, provision and protection. This is where the believer has reached spiritual maturity and enjoys a deep relationship with God.

If we read Psalm 91, which many Christians claim as protection in difficult times, such as during the Covid pandemic, we see how magnificently the Psalm is laid out. We see that God's protection is conditional based on being in a relationship of trust with Him. For instance, I can be concerned for the safety of all families during the outbreak of a virus, and I can communicate as much as I can what to do to prevent infection. But when it comes to my family, they are the ones I can best attend to because they are close to me and I can give them the best protection possible.

God's promise of protection in Psalm 91 is given to those who "Dwell in the shelter of the Most High" and "Rest in the shadow of the Almighty". It is administered to those "Who are under His wings" and who trust in Him. In the relationship God has with His people (His children or His wife), He promises to be faithful. Psalm 91:14 says: "Because he loves Me, says the Lord, I will rescue him" – which is the clearest depiction of a relationship and its mutual benefits. Verses 14 to 16 explain the pattern God followed with Old Testament Israel. Any modern-day believer will benefit from their relationship with God if they understand what Psalm 91 says about maintaining a relationship with God. People promote God's unconditional love as if He will put up with our unfaithfulness in our relationship with Him. It's just not true as we see when we correctly read John 3:16. In this remarkable verse we see that God loves the world, but He also gives eternal life (eternal friendship with Him) based on faith in His Son.

What God proposed to Israel – the blessings and related curses, the promises and benefits – was conditional for those maintaining their relationship with Him. We see the cycle of Israel walking with God and worshipping Him; being unfaithful to Him by wandering away through sin; God warning and then punishing them; Israel repenting and asking for forgiveness; and God forgiving them and restoring the relationship. The process God followed with Israel is the same for believers today. God is interested in building, developing and maintaining a relationship with every believer on earth, and His relationship with Israel is our example for life today. It is a 'practice-run' for what we see in the New Testament church and a format for eternity with God. We need to do battle with sin and its devastating effects on relationships. In doing so, we will ready ourselves for eternity with God where sin is non-existent and our relationships will last for ever.

The relational door

Israel was the nation of God, and it was God's intention that they be freed from slavery so that they might worship Him in the land He promised them – the place where He would live among the sheep of His pasture. Yet He did not march them out of Egypt until the price for sin was paid by the blood sacrifice of a lamb on the doorposts of every house. To be the people of God meant they needed to go through this specific 'act'. After their departure from slavery, God met with them at Mount Sinai and gave them His commandments that reflected His holy and righteous nature, and were part of the process to transform them into a people distinct from the nations around them. If they obeyed the commandments, it would transform them into God's holy nature and character. Israel's journey to the Promised Land was characterised by a fellowship between them and God. What allowed this fellowship was the blood on their doorposts on the night of their departure and their obedience to the laws and decrees of God.

In Romans 10:4, Paul says Christ is the end of the Law so that there may be righteousness for everyone who believes. He is saying that if we are saved by the grace of the Lord Jesus Christ, the righteous requirements of God are fulfilled in us through Jesus' obedience. Jesus living within us signifies our righteousness. Jesus has achieved a fulfilment of the entire Law. It is the 2 Corinthians 5:21 'divine exchange.' We received Jesus' righteousness and He received our unrighteousness. This new righteousness is the door that leads to our relationship with God. Sin, which brings separation, previously closed this relational door. This new friendship with God requires 'right-standing with God' before a friendship with God can be established. For us it is not the blood of a lamb (or goat), nor the laws of Israel that opens the door to fellowship with God, it is the blood of Jesus and our faith in the blood that washes away our sins.

Human worth

Why did God come to seek and save a lost people on a planet somewhere in the vast expanse of the universe? A planet full of people who, instead of worshipping Him, abandon Him.

The only reason we can offer is that creating mankind was an expression of God's love – this same love caused God to pursue mankind after his sinful rebellion. It is the love a father has for his children; God would do anything, once separated from them, to restore them to Himself. The connection is what made God pursue mankind, or said another way, it was God's intended friendship with humanity. When love creates, it never abandons; love always forgives and seeks restoration. In this book I have made it clear that true love can only exist in a relationship, and it is within the relationship God has with mankind that true love exists, and causes God to pursue mankind daily. It is the reason God considered it worth sending His own Son to die for the restoration of His children back to Himself. The true heart of a father is shown when He is willing to sacrifice His own Son as a demonstration of human worth to Him.

Denying what we were destined for

If I read Genesis chapters 1 to 3, and then read Revelation chapters 21 and 22, I clearly see God's intentions for mankind. No other book accurately reveals God's intentions, His will, and His ways as the Bible does. Many people deny its authority, but funnily enough, many movies have the same storyline as Scripture. A dominant theme in movies is the struggle between good and bad, light and dark; with a hero who saves the day. Another theme is romance between two people who fall in love. Even legal systems in developed and undeveloped countries are based on the Biblical principles of justice and consequences.

Despite mankind's attempts to deny the authority of the Bible in their lives, God's intention to create people to relationally exist with their Creator has been clear from the start. Scripture is God's way of explaining Himself and His intentions to us. Even if an unbeliever denies the authenticity of Scripture and its impact on his life, his life is still governed by who God is and what He does. Genesis tells us where we come from and Revelation tells us where we are going. Scripture makes it clear that we were destined to be with God, which means to be relationally joined to Him – not distant from Him. We are also warned about the dangers of becoming increasingly busy and of the distractions designed to prevent us from developing our relationship with God. This world and what is in it will cause us to exist eternally apart from God.

Our Creator's plan was and will forever be to inhabit a specially prepared place with the people who love Him.

When we read Psalm 42, we are given a glimpse of the author's longing to be with God his Creator. The author says his soul thirsts for the Lord, using the metaphor of a deer panting for water. The metaphor describes how only water can satisfy the deer's need – nothing else will do. This Psalm tells us how we were created to look to God for all we need. Should the deer not get the much-needed water, it would die. The author tells us that he, like us, is the deer in desperate need of water, which is the presence of God. Once we have found this source of all life, nothing else will suffice.

As believers, we cannot deny that we have the same longing deep within us. It is when we have tried all options around us to fulfil the longing within us that we realise only God can bring true lasting companionship. He is the One who purposed us to be His friends. Denying this is denying what we were destined for. Nothing in this world can quench the longing in our hearts the way God can. He made us to be dependent on Him for what only He can supply – His friendship and fellowship.

Part Three

Taking the steps

Chapter 8

Trust is at the heart

Trust is at the heart of all relationships. It binds the parties to an agreement or relationship together. We can define the word 'trust' as a firm belief in the reliability, truth or ability of someone or something. In the context of God's Word, we trust what is written in Scripture because we believe it is God Himself speaking to us. Paul says Scripture has its origin with God's Spirit, although it was penned by men (2 Timothy 3:16). We as believers rely on God's Word for our everything. We believe there is no other book or manual of traditions passed on from one generation to the other that can be compared and relied on apart from Scripture.

When we place our trust in God's Word, we place our trust in the person of God Himself and vice versa. God cannot be separated from His Word, which informs us about Himself – we will do well to develop a deep knowledge of God's Word and nurture a personal relationship with God. This means we can hear God and speak to Him. Most of us find it easier to speak to God than to hear Him for ourselves; His voice does not develop at the moment of justification, it is a process we have to invest and persist in. The more we have of God's Word in us, the easier it is for us to hear His voice. God, His voice and His Word agree. Our trust should be anchored unwaveringly in all three of these at the same time. God cannot lie or deceive, nor can He make a mistake or decide to abandon us, which would be going against His own Word. God remains the eternal sovereign God who can be trusted at all times. He has gone beyond promising us a secure future; He has sworn an oath in His own name to uphold what He has said.

Trust, on mankind's side of our relationship with God, can resemble the frayed end of a woven rope. Mankind is the one part of the relationship where trust is not certain. Not a day goes by where people do not violate their own promises. On God's side of the relationship with us, He can always be trusted.

A relationship exists where trust from both parties in the relationship is established. Each party in a relationship relies on the faithfulness of the other party to uphold their commitment. To better explain the founding role trust plays in any relationship, I want to use the example of composite glues. When you open the packet containing the glue, you find two separate components that need to be mixed before the glue can be applied to join the intended parts. In the same way, a relationship can only exist if both parties bring their trust to the agreement. This trust means, "When I enter the relationship – I put my trust in you and I can be trusted." While God is always faithful, it is mankind who is not.

We as believers expect God to remain faithful while we are the ones who transgress by breaking the trust. We say we will trust in what God says, but we allow ourselves to slip in and out of trust. Even in the Old Testament, we see how God describes His relationship with Israel. His Word depicts Israel as an unfaithful wife and God as the husband, which means that God, time and time again, has to forgive. To fully appreciate how much we can trust God, we need to understand and appreciate God's grace.

Redemption or relationship?

What must be emphasised at this stage is that salvation is an action towards the restoration of the relationship between God and every individual. Salvation is not the main goal in God's eternal plan. As important as it is, it is one step in the process of a fully restored friendship with God.

When God redeemed Israel from Pharaoh's clutches, Pharaoh paid with the death of his firstborn so that the children of God could walk free. That same night the blood of lambs that was applied to every Jewish household was the sign for the angel to pass over the Israelites' sin. They were protected against God's judgement by the blood of the sacrificial lamb. This was the first stage of God's plan of salvation for Israel. But God did not stop there.

We are excited when we see people getting saved. However, what they are saved into and what we teach them is their next step in God's plan for them. In many, cases people are basically sold a 'fire insurance policy' against the coming wrath of God. They are told that if they believe they are saved and 'safe'.

In many cases, it seems as if we make God's plan of redemption our focus in Scripture. We bring people out of slavery to sin and we leave them because we tell them that they are 'free' now. Is the blood on the doorposts – the cross of Christ – all they need to know? Similarly, is God's rescue plan of mankind expressed in a single event or do we see a deeper narrative in the Bible? Although redemption is an important theme in Scripture, we need to understand that it is a means to an end.

In the beginning, through Adam's sin, all of mankind was affected and lost God's presence and fellowship. In Genesis 3:15, God tells Satan, "I will put enmity between you and the woman, and between your seed and her Seed; he shall bruise your head, and you shall bruise his heel." This was a redemptive process instituted by God to restore relations between Himself and mankind.

We understand that fellowship with God existed before sin entered humanity and separated them from God. The process of a God-seed being born through a woman was necessary for the removal of sin. If this was to be accomplished, the result would be the reinstatement of relations between God and mankind. What was lost therefore, at the moment of sin, was again made available to all of humanity at the cross of Christ, and this was accomplished by the God-seed being born of a woman. Whoever believes in this redemption can be reunited with God through the process of adoption.

Redemption represents the atoning of Jesus for the sin of the world (John 3:16). The key to understanding John 3:16 is to look at what love is, what love did and why God had to send His Son to die for man's sin. We need to investigate what the Biblical narrative reveals regarding man's existence before the fall in Genesis 3. Here we see that mankind was in a relationship with God before the entrance of sin, and it was through sin that this relationship was damaged and required restoration through God's plan of redemption. What then, we need to ask, was the purpose of God's plan of redemption?

The moment sin entered the world through man's disobedience, the love God had for the people He created was not lost. Christ dying on the cross was God reassuring mankind of his love. God is love and therefore love has been in existence for as long as God exists.

Love can be found where more than one person exists – in the Trinity. God existed in a loving relationship before He created mankind and out of this relationship God created mankind to have a meaningful relationship with. God's focus after creating mankind was to fellowship with the person into whom He put His own breath of life. God did not create man to abandon him, but to walk with him every day (Genesis 3:8).

The connection between God and Adam was a relationship God Himself designed and established. This same desire for fellowship caused God to express His love by sending Jesus to die on the cross to restore the lost relationship with mankind after the entrance of sin. God's desire to walk with mankind is still as strong as the day in the Garden of Eden.

The plan of redemption is critical in the life of every person on earth. It was a plan designed for both heaven and earth, to solve the problem that rebellion created. Yet, if we focus solely on God's plan of redemption, we will miss what was in place between God and man before sin entered. If we ignore what Adam had with God before he fell into sin, we will develop a mindset of viewing redemption as a life insurance policy to enter heaven one day. We need to ask ourselves why God wanted to atone for sin.

We only have to read the beginning and the end of the Bible to see what God's plan was and still is. He wants to be with His people, and He wants them to be with Him forever and beyond time.

If we make the redemption theme the main focus, we fail to see the relationship God desires to have with each one of us. Jesus suffered and died not just to remove our sin, but to establish our reconnection with our heavenly Father. John expresses this well in John 1:12, where he says that those who believe in God are restored to fellowship with God as our Father. We therefore need to readjust our focus – from redemption to relations. The one is an intervention, while the other is a permanent intention.

The Greatest Commandment

In the previous section we saw the journey God took Israel on to fulfil the promise of salvation made to Abraham. As part of this journey, we also saw that God gave Israel the Ten Commandments. In Exodus 20:1-2 we see that God starts with a declaration of His grace and love for His people. In the next portion, from verse 3-17, we see the terms and conditions of the covenant God made with Israel, which come 'packaged' in love. Love is what enables us to obey, love is what makes us want to obey, love is what makes us obey God as we reciprocate His love shown to us. For this reason, the greatest commandment is to love the Lord your God and your neighbour as yourself (Deuteronomy 6:5 and Mark 12:29). This command is found in the Old and New Testament.

The best place to gain an understanding of what love truly is, is to see what God has revealed in Scripture. The Bible tells us what God did in sending His Son to die for sinful man – to reconcile mankind back to God. This understanding informs our thinking about how we are to live our lives concerning God and others; sacrificing what is important to us, treating others with kindness

70

and humility, and putting others first and doing what is best for them.

Paul explains this when he uses the analogy of a marriage in Ephesians 5:22-33. This love relationship ties in with being faithful, obedient, humble, and not self-seeking – all of which resemble the fruit of the Spirit. In Jeremiah 3:20 God speaks to Old Testament Israel and addresses her as His 'wife'. A marriage symbolises protection and provision and is governed by a covenant. The marriage God refers to is His relationship with Israel. Covenantal faithfulness means devotion to only *one*, not multiple partners or many different gods. In Deuteronomy 6:4-25, the Shema stipulates the commands of God that govern His relationship with Israel. It also details the nature and person of God. We see in it that God expects from Israel a single focus and devotion. They are to love God only and serve no other gods or idols. The Shema presents a similar set of vows to the ones a husband and wife make to each other on the day of their marriage. It is a promise to be faithful to each other even unto death.

The Shema

In Matthew 22:34-40 we read an amazing encounter. The Pharisees decided to do a Q&A with Jesus to test Him. They wanted Him to falter in public so they could gather evidence against Him that could lead towards a successful prosecution. "Teacher, which is the greatest commandment in the Law?" They expected a legalistic reply, but instead, Jesus begins with "love". This is the same principle explained by God in Exodus 20:1-2 before He introduced the Ten Commandments to Israel at Mount Sinai. Jesus answers, we are to love God and love our neighbour. His explanation, as the one in Exodus 20, puts love at the centre of all we do.

It calls us to reciprocate God's love shown towards us. It is a love that commands our volitional obedience and at the same time it is a response from the heart of every believer towards the holiness of the ONE eternal God.

In its entirety, the Shema consists of three paragraphs: Deuteronomy 6:4–9, Deuteronomy 11:13–21 and Numbers 15:37–41. It is the commands God gave Israel and it forms the basis of Israel's morning and evening prayers. Traditionally it is a Jewish person's last words on earth. The Shema allows Israel to demonstrate their love for God by observing His commands.

Jesus continues His answer to the Pharisees by saying all the Law and the Prophets, meaning the Old Testament, hang on these two commands of love for God and our neighbour. This means if we were to remove love from the commandments God gave to Israel, we would end up with a set of cold hard laws, similar to other religions.

Because God is love, removing love removes the person of God from the Law. His person is love, which is the very thing He demonstrated when He rescued His people from slavery. Their obedience was to be a response to what He has done for them. Jesus' answer in Matthew 22 upheld what God said to Israel in Exodus 20. He was speaking relationally; explaining that love can only exist within the context of a relationship.

However, the Pharisees, with their cold legalistic mindset, missed what Jesus was saying. In their view, their legalistic observation of Torah was all God desired. What was missing on their side was the transforming love that birthed obedience within their hearts. Love births obedience; not the other way round. They were harsh followers of the Law, but even the 'chief' Pharisee, Saul (later known as Paul), acknowledged that harsh treatment of the body cannot stop sin (Colossians 2:23). Through the Pharisees' lack of understanding, they made observation of the Law the key to acceptance by God, and while they pursued this ideology, they were unable to receive God's love. This in turn prevented them from showing love to others. Their murderous plans to eliminate Jesus were clear evidence of this. People have created many sets of religious laws over centuries, but until we understand that love is the key to right-standing with God, we will perpetually try to work harder to earn God's approval through the observation of laws. Within the Trinity, love personifies God as He expresses His relational nature by demonstrating love to a sinful world.

Chapter 9

Pursue what is of greater worth

Jesus did not hold onto His place in heaven, but chose to leave it, to give it all up to win it all. He gave up His prized position to gain it all. He was after the relationship, not the position. He was willing to forego the throne to secure what was more important. He gave up His place on the throne for something on earth. That something is the relationship between God the Trinity, which was expressed in the relationship seen between God and man.

When Jesus said: "Turn the other cheek; or give your coat," He was hinting at the ability to forego a prized possession to gain or restore a relationship. Jesus, in His Sermon on the Mount, turned everything upside down. He spoke for humility and against power. He taught about being gentle and weak instead of being proud and arrogant. He said the poor have a special place before God. He advocated that we should not hold onto lesser things when we can gain eternal things.

By foregoing worldly possessions, power and prestige, we set our sights on things of eternal value. His sermon that day still resounds loudly today. Jesus was saying we should shun what God shuns and embrace what He embraces. We need to understand what God values and act accordingly. Jesus' teaching introduced people to what it will be like when God comes to live and walk among His people. His sermon explained how God sees us linked to a relationship with Him and with others.

In Luke 12, Jesus is teaching a crowd of several thousand people, when a man interrupted and asked Jesus to tell his brother to share the inheritance between them as brothers. Jesus addressed the request by saying, in verses 15-21, a man's life does not consist of the abundance of his possessions, but how rich he is towards God. God has no desire for earthly riches and mankind cannot take any of their possessions to heaven. We learn that it is far better to build a relationship with God, apart from earthly possessions. This relationship takes man to heaven and follows man into heaven.

The risk in material possession it that they can prevent us from building a relationship with God. Ultimately, they get old and suffer damage and so do we when we realise we have lost out on eternal life with God. What is of greater value is the relationship with God – first and foremost. Possessions in themselves are a God-given blessing if they are treated in the way Jesus explains: they are to serve us – not us serve them.

In verse 21 Jesus says we are to gather for ourselves treasures in heaven. This, He says, is to be rich towards God. How do we gather heavenly treasures? It begins with growing a relationship with God. Out of this relationship all life flows. Within this relationship we are taught what to do and what not to do. Living our lives in a way that pleases God does not constitute a legalistic right and wrong. No such cold obedience is fulfilling. What fulfils a man's heart is to obey God from a heart filled with love. When we embrace the love of God, our relationship with Him begins to grow. Out of this relationship, functioning happens. We begin to hear, see and understand what God wants us to do. We begin to discern, like Jesus, what, where and when we are to act on His behalf. What pleases the Father most is if we do only what He says – nothing more and nothing less. This was Jesus' testimony in John 14:10.

If we grasp the importance of putting God above all possessions on earth, we also realise the great wealth in our relationships with one another. In this passage, the two brothers are obviously caught up in an argument over their late father's decision regarding His will. We often see how a good and healthy relationship between siblings is marred when their inheritance, after their father's passing, is not what they expected. Not only are their earthly relationships harmed, but also their relationship with God.

If we pursue what is of greater worth, we need to train our hearts and minds to live above the pleasures, attractions, and desires of this world. So many things around us are designed to be distractions – keeping us from being "rich towards God." These distractions steal our valuable time and before we know it, we are caught in a web of arguments with others and we lose sight of the love of God expressed in relationships.

Sacrificing worldly possessions and pleasures for the sake of building relationships with God and others is worth it all.

True obedience

The Bible is a story of true love. It also contains many important commands. If taken out of their context, they could become hard rules that people enforce on others and themselves. These hard rules often hurt people and can destroy relationships. Are we called by God to just obey His commands or face annihilation? Or do we obey God's commands because we want to reciprocate His unending love for us.

In Proverbs 3:3 we see love and faithfulness mentioned. If we miss the context of Proverbs, we could apply these two principles in a legalistic way and demand their strict adherence. But if we place them within the story where God gave these principles, through Solomon, in order to maintain the relationship between Him and Israel, then we have placed them within their proper context to understand and follow. We see that love, faithfulness and obedience do not operate as standalone principles; they function within the framework of a relationship.

In John 16, Jesus said, "If you love Me you will obey my commandments." If Jesus makes this strong connection between love and obedience, what is the essence of true obedience?

In trying to understand the link Jesus made between obedience and love, I found obedience to be an act of compliance with an order, a request, or law, or submitting myself to another's authority. True obedience is trust in another person of higher authority; laying down my own opinion and submitting to the person's higher knowledge. Obedience has nothing to do with wealth, position or status. It requires the same "laying down of the will" from anyone. Interestingly, when I obey I always benefit from it. Obedience must come from a free will – the same as disobedience. The Spirit helps us make the right choices by showing us how we will benefit from obeying God's righteous decrees. We see from Scripture that the reward for obedience is life. The opposite is also true. The reward for disobedience is death.

Obedience, when seen in the context of a Biblical figure like Abraham, means to abandon everything man can do and gather for himself and pursuing what God can supply and provide. Abraham left his home, his place of surety, his known for the unknown. The important thing is that Abraham had God as his friend wherever he went.

In the passage on the greatest commandment, I showed that Exodus 20:1-2 declares the love of God for His people, and Exodus 20:3-17 gives the Ten Commandments. This means that our obedience, fulfilling His righteous requirements, is in response to what God has already done for us. This is what John 14:15 says, namely: Obedience to God's commands is a way of thanksgiving for His plan of redemption – of which we are the beneficiaries.

Jesus obeying His Father's request to die for the sins of mankind is one of the greatest examples of obedience for us to follow. Jesus' obedience came with a big sacrifice. He had to lay down His heavenly privileges and adopt a lower existence, but in doing so His focus was to achieve a long-term goal. After being incarnated as a man, Jesus died, was buried, resurrected and glorified to the highest position next to His Father in heaven. Our focus should be similar. The call to obedience should not only be a calculation of our immediate sacrifices, or the letting go of our own desires; it should be a reciprocation of God's grace and love for sending us

His Son to die in our place for our wrongs – paying the penalty we should have paid. To reciprocate means we show our gratitude by doing what God asks us to do. Both the accounts in Exodus 20:1-17 and John 14:15 show God's reciprocation expectations. Amazingly, He even empowers us to reciprocate His grace and love by giving us His Holy Spirit who enables us to walk in His commands (Ezekiel 36:27).

This principle of God taking the first step towards us and then allowing us to respond to His grace and love by obeying His commandments is what forms the basis of our relationship with Him. In fact, the commandments He gives us to follow are moral principles full of wisdom that are for our benefit, our health and for eternal life. Hidden within them is God's wisdom that always promotes righteousness, joy and peace. These commandments only seem difficult or limiting when we perceive them without love. When we come to the understanding that God rescued us from a raging torrent of sin and death, only then do we realise that we cannot dictate the terms of our relationship with God. Jesus explains this in Luke 7:47 where He says the person who has been forgiven much will love much.

True obedience is therefore our response to God's love. He saw enough in us to count us worthy of His Son's sacrificial death. Is His sacrifice on our behalf not worth considering?

Relational ignorance

What is ignorance in the context of a relationship? A relationship can be a place of both incredible testing and unimaginable fulfilment. A relationship can expose wrong expectations and reveal the true intent of people's hearts. Relationships can cause us to act out good or bad things that we ourselves don't know we are capable of. People who have been married for decades display a love and a faithfulness towards each other in the face of difficult circumstances.

On the other hand, what began as happy marriage ceremonies can turn into mere survival, because of verbal and physical abuse. We see this daily, and it is, unfortunately, our frame of reference, and it can shape our expectations of who God is and how He treats those He loves. The worldview of human to human rela- tionships we grow up with (the horizontal view) erroneously shapes our expectation of what we should expect and how we should behave when we enter a vertical relationship (God to mankind). We don't have an example of relational perfection in this world, and what we have suffered in our lives becomes our canvas for what we attempt to portray about who God is and what He is like.

We can learn volumes about relationships by studying docu- mented relationships that educate, prepare and inform us what we can expect and how we are to conduct ourselves. One of our greatest weaknesses and the reason we fall into and out of so many relationships, is that we want to understand God and relate to him based on our knowledge and relational experiences on earth. We project a God we do not know onto a cinema screen based on what we experience socially. Our homes, workplaces, business dealings, and friendships all form part of how we expect God to be and how He will treat us. Our expectations are based on a severe lack of knowledge of who God truly is and how He treats those who walk with Him. If we are honest, we would have to admit that we are ignorant regarding God. This means we begin to relate to God based on what we grow up with. We want to dictate the conditions of the friendship and when we do not get what we want, we frame God as the culprit.

We do this because what we experience in relationships here on earth are fragments of something astounding, brilliant and pure that once existed. Metaphorically speaking, it resembles a historic remnant of an ancient city, renowned for its architectural and engineering marvels. Today we look at it and are wowed by it, yet we do not fully grasp the creative designs, its culture, the traditions, practices and work ethic that went into the construction of the city and its surroundings. By studying the remains of an ancient city, we are able to glean how it worked and we gain some knowledge of the city's history. But unless we can meet the designers of the city, our knowledge will always fall short of what went into the design and construction of the city. A lack of in-depth knowledge will always distort our future expectations. If the ancient fathers of those impressive marvels documented their thoughts, perhaps we would know more about how to design such impressive cities today.

When we read Scripture, we are well informed by the Father of creation, who documented His thoughts regarding His friendships with mankind. The life and experiences of the man called Job are available to us. Job is one of the oldest books in the Bible. He lived about the same time as the patriarch, Abraham, and it gives us a glimpse of what a close relationship with God is like. Reading this book, we are able to nullify wrong expectations of who God is and what He is like. Job, being a man like us, tells us what we can expect when walking relationally with God. Job lived in the age of the Patriarchs and he had several personal encounters with God. His relationship with God teaches us some key aspects of who God is, what He does, and how He treats those He loves. It also describes the fate of those who despise Him. The interactions between God and Job give us an in-depth understanding of how God expresses His love to those who follow Him.

The book of Job certainly reveals several misnomers in our knowledge of God and His dealings with mankind. Scripture depicts Job as a man who was, "Blameless and upright, who feared God and shunned evil." Job 1:1 tell us this about this remarkable man, and verses two and three tell us he was the "greatest of all the people in the East." He was wealthy, well known and respected by many. Why would Job choose to fear God and shun evil? From the start of this book, we see that, unlike many who fall in love with wealth, Job's life-focus was his relationship with God and not his possessions, nor his position in society. These two aspects, throughout history, have driven many people away from God. We see how Job's devotion to God allowed him to maintain his relationship with God, despite his wealth, status, or severe suffering. Job reveals how his friendship with God was based on his knowledge of God, which lead to a deep trust and reliance on God, and how this was in sharp contrast to his friends' and even his wife's ignorance of God.

In Hosea 4:6, the prophet made a remarkable statement. God instructed him to tell Israel, "My people are destroyed from lack of knowledge." The knowledge God was referring to was not worldly knowledge, it was and still is the knowledge of God, which is eminently higher than all other knowledge. This knowledge refers to revelations from God Himself. It is a knowledge we get from reading the Word and the illumination of our understanding that the Holy Spirit gives – it sustains the believer.

This knowledge, that God says His people lack, is a 'knowing' more excellent than all of man's wisdom and scientific discoveries.

Mankind's knowledge is what we get when eating from the Tree of Knowledge of Good and Evil; it is mankind's volitional disobedience to God's commands as we foolishly pursue an already condemned existence (Genesis 2:16-17). God commanded Adam not to eat from the Tree of Knowledge of Good and Evil, but rather from the Tree of Life.

In the New Testament, Jesus described eternal life in John 17:3 as knowing God. The explanation given by the Son of God is that eternal life means to know God. To know God suggests a close intimacy, just as a husband and wife are intimate in marriage (Genesis 4:1). It indicates experiential knowledge, not theoretical or head knowledge. In Amos 5:4, God says: "Seek Me and live!" To "Seek Me" means a day-to-day walking together; it means to live as Jesus did. By walking with God we gain experiential knowledge of Him, which becomes an intimate knowing of Him. His Spirit will guide our understanding to what He likes and dislikes. We grow in this relational knowledge by reading and understanding His Word. The Spirit uses the Word of God written on our hearts to guide us to walk as Jesus did. This 'knowing' develops deeper in us daily, and it is crucial because eternal life is for those who intimately know Him and have walked with Him relationally. While academic knowledge cannot develop a relationship, daily interaction does.

In Philippians 3:8, Paul says he counts all other things loss for the excellence of the knowledge of God. The rejection of knowledge, the prophet Isaiah says, results in captivity (Isaiah 5:13). The captivity Isaiah refers to, is seen when mankind, because of their lack of knowledge of God's will and His ways, falls back onto their own way of thinking and reasoning. Mankind becomes their own source of knowledge. This is the core reason why God commanded Adam not to eat from the Tree of Knowledge of

Good and Evil (Genesis 2:16-17). When the knowledge of God is absent, every person does as they see fit (Judges 21:25). In a leadership context, it is the blind leading the blind.

The more distant mankind lives from the knowledge of God, the more they begin to live closer to the ways of the devil. It is a process during which people's thinking is slowly re-programmed to shun all knowledge from and about God and His ways. Mankind puts their trust in their own abilities and their own so-called truths. An example of this is science's 'big bang theory' a belief in the *zeitgeist*. The big bang is science's theory of the origin of life, which is both theoretically and heretically anchored in an atheistic ideology.

The *zeitgeist* is a general intellectual, moral, and cultural climate of an era, with the theory that you can experience your here and now; you can own your own reality. The *zeitgeist*, the spirit of the age, ignores the past. It places mankind at the forefront of their own existence and moves God completely out of the way. What the serpent purported in the Garden of Eden to Adam and Eve (Genesis 3:3-5) was similar to what science and *zeitgeist* followers advocate. It is a different knowledge to that of God's; it is fruit taken from the Tree of Knowledge of Good and Evil. It brings death, not life. During the temptation of mankind, the serpent could only promote 'knowledge', not life (Genesis 3:5). Knowledge can be inanimate without ever bringing or sustaining life. The devil did not present it as his own, he only had to get them to walk away from the knowledge of God in order to destroy them. Scripture is clear that there is no 'other' knowledge to sustain mankind, but the knowledge of God.

Ignorance of the knowledge of God causes man to fear. The moment mankind was disobedient to God, they became naked

(Genesis 3:7). Their Godly covering was gone in an instant and their best attempt at restoration was to sew fig leaves together. Today we see how mankind sews their own fig leaves when they try to come up with answers to life and the universe.

Without knowing that God loves this world and the people He created, mankind speculates on God's intentions. They argue who and what God is and they question His existence. People's ignorance of God makes them write their own theories on what God is like and what He wants from mankind. They create arguments and explanations why He is autonomous, and debate why they can self-regulate and survive on their own knowledge. Humanity makes themselves the judge, the justifier, and the accused, and wear the coats of the physician and the patient. After man's fall, God initiated dialogue with man, and Adam's comments revealed what the loss of the knowledge of God does (Genesis 3:8-10). When mankind walks away from the knowledge of God, they are filled with fear, suspicion and distrust.

We see how people today have a distorted view of God. Some acknowledge His existence with either anger and or great frustration. They know He exists but resent Him for not helping in their struggles. Others choose to 'go it alone'. Whether people are agnostic, theistic or atheistic, they believe they will find the meaning of life. To many, it is to be happy and live a good life, while to others, life is a struggle and then you die. Death to them is similar to falling asleep every night – the only difference is that you never wake up again.

Another ideology exists where people are void of the knowledge of God. They believe God exists, that He is compassionate, and that He wants to be involved in their lives, bringing peace, happiness and fulfilment. Yet they are unable to find the correct way of getting His attention. Without possessing the correct knowledge, they begin to work for their salvation. They begin to 'do in order to achieve'. This is how the corporate world functions. Doing more gets you acknowledged, and once you have been acknowledged, you are promoted to a higher status. Status is achieved through performance. The one big problem with working or doing in order to achieve, is that you have no prescribed set of rules. You design and amend as you go, based on your own subjective worldview and philosophy.

The reality is that whether you find yourself in the camp of those denying God's existence or you are working to be accepted by God, you are equally ignorant and void of eternal life. Your life is filled with suspicion and uncertainty. You confuse joy and happiness and perpetually seek rest that is out of your reach.

In God is rest, fulfilment, acceptance and salvation from a broken world. In Him is true knowledge that sets us free from our own pathetic attempts to self-regulate and self-perfect. When we are able to seek after God, we begin to receive His revealed knowledge – that He loves us; that He died for us to liberate us from sin; that He wants to be with us and us with Him. It settles the burning desire in mankind to be accepted and valued.

Ignorance of who God is and what He expects of us cause us to work harder and harder to earn God's favour. It blinds us from knowing He has already provided all we need to be restored to our Creator; to the One who loves us. Relational ignorance destroys nations and causes people to experience hell on earth. Life without God was never God's intention. It is one of the devil's sneakiest investment schemes he sells. Relational ignorance tells people that either God does not exist and that we need to go it alone, or it lies and tells us that God is unapproachable during our times of need and that He is cold and distant.

Check and check again

The greatest weakness mankind has is a lack of revelatory Scriptural knowledge, which is detrimental to our spiritual development. It is prevalent among believers who make assumptions and incorrect connections based on Scriptural passages they string together. Problems occur through incorrect interpretation of Scripture, when believers use a one-off event as guidance for multiple situations in their lives, and when patterns in Scripture are ignored.

An example is in Luke 23:43, which relates Jesus' words to the thief hanging next to Him on the cross. This man was a convicted criminal who found salvation moments before his death. He was not a witness for Christ during any part of his life, except in his penitent confession, particularly compared with the convict on the other side of Jesus. The Old Testament pattern is Freedom from Egyptian Slavery, the Wilderness Walk, and finally entry and residence in the Promised Land. The pattern found in the New Testament is justification, sanctification and finally glorification. We cannot deny the thief's justification before his death, but this single event, detailed in Scripture, cannot be taken as a pattern for us all. During his life he didn't know Jesus. By the grace of Christ, this man's faith on the cross was enough to secure his entry into heaven. However, we are not to follow this once-off event. It was meant to show God's salvation grace to the richest man as well as to the most hardened criminal. We are meant to follow the pattern found in Scripture that details salvation as a journey to meet God and grow in a deep relationship with Him.

Unfortunately, many believers will emulate the salvation of the criminal who hung on the cross. Yes, he did get saved, but he did not invest in getting to know Jesus and the fellowshipping Spirit of God. We are to read the Scriptures correctly to ensure we check and check again what God expects from us. Making baseless assumptions and illegitimate connections will cost us dearly.

Chapter 10

Fruitfulness from intimacy

E very time I read the Psalmist's question (Psalm 8), I try to answer it for myself: what makes God mindful of man? Why is the Creator of the universe willing to suffer and die in order to remove the barrier of sin between God and man? Is there anything mankind can do or give God in exchange for what God has done for humanity? Mankind has no claim to deity, yet the Deity has given their own to save mankind from eternal destruction. To God, restoring the friendship between Deity and mortal man was worth taking extraordinary steps. The Deity we know as the Trinity not only planned before the foundations of the earth were established, but God also came to earth, pursuing mankind by taking on the body of a mortal man to achieve friendship between God and man.

God designed fruitfulness and increase to be the result of relational intimacy. This is clearly expressed when God Himself proclaimed the institution of marriage and children that are born from intimacy between the husband and his wife. In Genesis 1:28

God makes it clear that the relationship comes first and thereafter the increase. A loving relationship will bring forth loved children who can give love because they have experienced love. Any increase outside God's plan brings long-term pain. The God-ordained institution of a marriage, God's ultimate expression of 'relationship', is God's method for mankind's increase or reproduction.

Scripture informs us about the relationship within the Trinity. It also tells us of the relationships between God and man and man and man. Ever since the days of Adam and Eve, God has always been intimately involved in the lives of mankind. Acts 26 tells us that God even plans our existence on earth. His plan can be seen as He outworks it in the lives of men from creation until now. God's household is explained in many ways in Scripture, but the best of these is when Paul explains it as Christ being the bridegroom and the church being the bride (Ephesians 5:27). A closer, more loving and fruitful example would be difficult to find. John, on the island of Patmos, gives the same connotation in Revelation 19:7-9.

History is littered with false teachings and it is, unfortunately, possible for a person to stray from a loving relationship. Heresy is like a third illegitimate person entering a marriage, which causes the marriage to break up. The devil preached a false teaching to Adam and Eve in the Garden of Eden, and the result was a breakup in the relationship between God and mankind. Historically, false teachings have caused many people's relationship with God to end up on the rocks. Heresies either prescribe 'another gospel' or promote 'self-righteous' programmes, also known as 'do-it-yourself' courses. Others run parallel to the truth, but after a while gaping holes in their doctrine are visible for outsiders to see. One common factor, in all these 'other ways to get to God' is that they deny the person and work of Christ. It is through Christ alone that we can cry Abba Father. Only in Christ have we been given sonship. History is like a library, detailing the mistakes made by individuals who were taken on a detour by the devil's schemes and lies. Sadly, not many of them ever made it back. In 1 John 4:1-6, John gives us the tools to identify and avoid falsehood. We need these helpful tools in an era where knowledge and information permeate the airwaves and social media. The closer we stay to Jesus Christ, who is the truth, the easier it is for us to avoid being caught in a snare. Where do children run when danger approaches? They run to mommy and daddy. The same should apply to us.

A further aspect related to the fruitfulness we get from a healthy relationship is the fact that God partner's with mankind. When studying systematic theology and the doctrine of God, we learn that God does not need mankind to achieve His purposes. He exists apart from what He creates. He sovereignly acts independent from mankind. He is all powerful and sustains everything by the power of His Word. Despite this, He chooses to 'partner' with mankind to achieve certain objectives.

Examples from Scripture:

- God called Noah to build an ark to rescue the righteous.
- God called Abraham to be the father of Israel, the people of God.
- God called Moses, the lawgiver, to liberate and lead Israel.
- God used Judges to govern Israel.
- God partnered with men and women to defeat Israel's enemies, including Joshua, Deborah, Caleb, Nehemiah and others.

- God called David to shepherd His people.
- God tasked David and Solomon to design and build the Jerusalem temple.
- God called, equipped, and used prophets to speak His messages to His people.
- Jesus called His disciples to be trained and sent out to preach the Good News.
- The apostles, empowered by the Spirit of God, selflessly continued the work Jesus started.
- The Spirit of God gives gifts to people for works of service.
- The church today.

God could have achieved all these activities without the help of any person. What is interesting about these achievements, is that they are all by people who were called by God, and they had to trust and rely on Him to complete what they had been called to do. Faith was the key ingredient in all of them. Faith or trust is the cement in any relationship. Without it, any bond will crumble.

The list above is proof that the greater the work God calls a person to, the closer the person's relationship with God. The opposite is also true. Israel's first king, Saul, was called to a prominent position, yet the absence of a relationship with God saw him destroyed. Although the Pharisees were the ones who were to teach, govern and lead God's people, their focus was on the Law and its enforcement, and not on God. The lack of a close relationship with God in any leader's life causes the leader to dictate what they want from people. It distorts the office and task they have been given to fulfil and it enslaves the people. Israel's colourful history testifies to this fact. As long as Israel had a leader who followed after God, the nation flourished. When such a leader was replaced by a godless person, the nation suffered. We can therefore see from Scripture that, in order for a marriage to be healthy, or for a church to be a pillar and foundation of truth, the leadership has to walk with God. Fruitfulness comes from partnering with God. It is my personal view that God offered His all to us in the man Jesus, so that we will offer Him our all.

Perversion prevents fruitfulness

God imputed His relational characteristics into mankind at creation, which means that mankind, before the fall, was able to relate to God. Post the fall, mankind lost some of this ability, but not all. Where Adam related to his wife in a holy manner, which included intimacy, post the fall, mankind's relational ability was distorted. Love has been replaced by lust, which has driven mankind away from natural God-given relational boundaries. Man, since the days of Abraham and Lot, demonstrated perversions in their relationships.

Whatever God creates, wherever God is busy, Satan comes to distort and destroy. Having had a close relationship with God, familiarity set in and Satan became arrogant and proud and set his sights on God's throne. He valued a position more than a sustaining relationship. He was accused of rebellion and subordination and was kicked out of heaven and his intimate relationship with God. After suffering the losses, he set his sights on derailing the relationship between God and mankind.

Satan will do his best to prevent a person from getting saved, and if he fails in this step, he will do whatever he can to prevent the believer from developing a strong personal relationship with God. We can see from the beginning in Genesis how he employed clever strategies to distort every relationship. He succeeded in separating mankind from God and then set out to separate mankind from each other. From Cain killing his brother Abel to men chasing after men, Satan has targeted relationships – for one main reason. After God created man and placed him in the garden to be ruler over it, God commanded mankind to be fruitful and to multiply. Relationships are the carriers of fruitful expansion in all areas and when a relationship suffers perversion, it cannot be fruitful as God intended it to be. There can be increase, but that increase only leads to more perversion and eventual destruction.

To really know Him

Many people have said the apostles were the most privileged to have known, touched and walked with Jesus. In today's world, we do not have the privilege of sitting next to Jesus and touching Him. Yet, when addressing Thomas' unbelief, Jesus said (John 20:29) that we are more blessed if we believe in Him even though we have not seen Him.

The New Testament makes mention in many places that we are to "know Him ..." Here are some of them:

Philippians 3:10 / John 17:3 / Philippians 3:8

1 John 5:20 / 2 Peter 3:18 / 1 John 2:3

John 10:14 / 2 Peter 2:20 / 1 John 2:4

To know God through Jesus Christ and be assisted by the Spirit of God is the greatest blessing any person can receive. We might find that to truly know God could cost us everything in this world. Paul states, in Philippians 3:8, that he considers "everything a loss," compared with knowing Jesus. His "everything" was a costly step.

Knowing Jesus does not come cheaply in terms of worldly posses-sions, position and power.

1 John 5:18-20 says we are children of God, children who know God, and that we need "understanding" from God to know Him. Without this understanding we would only know God in an acad-emic way. The moment we begin to see God as far removed or distant, our obedience will begin to waiver. The opposite is also true. 1 John 2:4-6 says that knowing God is exemplified through our love for Him. How do we know we truly love Him? Our love is demonstrated by how much of His truth is in us and actively ordering our steps.

There are two levels of knowing a person. First, we know them through communication and sight. Second is the level of sharing what is present in their lives. Perhaps they suffer from an illness or an unexpected setback. Do I know what their pain is? Do I take time to investigate, not necessarily how to relieve their pain, but to show them I care?

Jesus shed tears for the sake of Jerusalem. He foresaw the suffering that was coming because she refused His salvation. Jesus travailed for the church unto death to set her free from the bondage of sin. He gave up His place next to the Father to suffer for those who were His enemies. Seated at the Father's throne, Jesus still intercedes for the bride He gave up His all for. True love is expressed in Ephesians 5:25-28 where Paul says a husband gives his all for his wife as Christ gave His all for His bride.

With this in mind, we need to ask ourselves whether we are affected by what affected Him historically and still affects Him. The sufferings He underwent are still present with us today. We see how His bride is seduced and ill-treated by a world that is inspired and driven by the forces of Satan. This prompts us to ask ourselves if we are in a self-serving relationship? Scripture says we are in Christ and He is in us. We therefore are deeply connected to Him, and if we tune into this relationship, we will sense His ongoing work against sin, death and the devil – not only in our own personal lives, but also in those who believe in Him and are still to believe in Him.

Above all, keep Him close

The theme of this book is putting God first. He is worth giving up all things that might stand in the way of worshipping Him. Our God is before all things and above all power, He is worth more than all the wealth the world can provide, He is more empowering than any position of power and He is above all other gods and above all nature and objects we can see.

God deserves to be first in all we are and do. How then, do we practically put God first in everything? Imagine walking into a shop and not having a list of what to buy. You walk around aimlessly trying to remember what to get. However, if you walk into a shop with a list, you are focused and you get what you came for. Without a list in a shop, you will suddenly crave certain foods; the lovely smell from the bakery section will overcome you; the items on special will scream at you, and you will fall victim to the sweets placed at the check-out area. You end up buying the wrong things and wasting money.

Every believer has to make a conscious decision what and with who they are in relationships with. The shopping list mentioned represents our needed focus on God's commands and His require-ments for our lives. Our obedience to these is what demonstrates our love for God. We need to inform ourselves what He approves of and disapprove of. If we create a mental list of what God requires of us, we will not resemble the shopper who shops aimlessly. The list will prevent us from getting distracted and tempted by items pleasing to the eye. These enticements are not necessarily bad, but they are being used by the great deceiver to lure us away from God to destroy the life-giving relationship God desires with us.

What are the distractions we are warned about and are they only found in our modern world? Is the devil not perhaps using the same old strategy he always uses to deceive all of mankind? The apostle John warns us against four things (1 John 2:16-17):

1. The cravings of sinful man.
2. The lust of what we see.
3. The boastful pride of what we have.
4. The boasting of what we achieve.

These things could become long-term distractions in our lives and prevent us from walking close to God. Since the fall of man, the strategies the enemy employs to deceive and distract man from the presence of God have not changed – they are as relevant today as they were in Genesis 3:6.

Satan uses those four things to draw us away from God. His aim is for us to fall in love with this world instead of God. Through these four things, we join ourselves to the world, we build dreams and commit our lives to achieving them. But beware, if they begin to rule our lives, no meaningful relationship can be established with God. John says that loving the world and the things it offers oppose the love for and of the Father in us (1 John 2:15). He says these worthless and temporary things we are so easily captivated by cause us to lose our eternal life. In 1 John 3, the apostle repeats the warning that sin stops us from a deep meaningful relationship with God. We are to cultivate our relationship with God by prioritising time with Him – putting Him first in our daily calendar. If we put Him first, all other temptations and distractions will become of no value to us. Jesus Himself, in Luke 12:35-48 gave a stark warning about this. In the relational context of a master and his servants, Jesus says we need to stay focused on what the Master desires from us. In this way we will not suffer loss or punishment when He suddenly arrives and requests a report from us.

The litmus test

How do we evaluate the health of our relationship with God? The apostle John gives us a litmus test to do this. His test reveals how crucial our relationships with God is. John places the parameters of the test as either life or death. The test for relational health is, "Do we love our neighbour as we love ourselves?" If we love our neighbour, John says, we have eternal life within us. If we do not love our neighbour, we remain in death and darkness (1 John 3:14). He makes love very practical and says if God's love is in us, we will look after our brothers. This action on our part will reveal if love is in us or not. A relationship with God therefore reveals if we are able to love our neighbour. The love we have for our neighbour is a reflection of the depth of love we have for God.

In 1 John 3:23-24, the apostle makes a direct link between the love we have for God, our obedience to His commands, and our relationship with each other. God's command is to love one another. If we obey this, we demonstrate our love for God through our obedience. Love acts as an encouragement to assist us to be obedient. In the same chapter of 1 John, in verse 24, he says that obeying God shows our relational love for Him. The litmus test of being in a relationship with God is, 'do we love our neighbour?' The first fruit of the Spirit of God is love. Therefore, loving our neighbour reveals if we have the Holy Spirit within us. It is for this reason that a relationship with God is primary to developing a relationship with our neighbour.

Is it not amazing that when we get closer to God, His love is shed abroad in our hearts and we begin to love and care about others – perhaps something we have not done before? We will find that our own personal stories and our likes and dislikes will not be selfish and self-centred anymore. We will be turned to focus on the lives of others. If we look for true fulfilment in this world, it won't be what we ourselves have done or achieved, but the legacies we have left in the lives of others. We see the richest people in the world, those who have sacrificed their all to achieve fame and fortune, giving back to others. People call this the "spirit of the universe." It is the heart and nature of the One who created the universe – our God and our ever-present companion.

The role of the Spirit of God

In John 16:7 Jesus said to His disciples, "It is for your good that I am going away. Unless I go away, the Helper [Advocate] will not come to you."

Jesus, being God, was incarnated on earth. His movements and abilities were hampered by His physical body. He could not deal with all the people He wanted to, and what's more, He could not change them from the inside as the prophet foretold in Ezekiel 36:27. Jesus had to leave in order for the Holy Spirit to come and indwell the hearts of every believer.

The Holy Spirit and Jesus have been directly involved in the process of reconciling man back to God. In other words, both

Jesus and the Holy Spirit were needed to restore the friendship between God and mankind. Both are doing for us and in us what we are unable to do for ourselves. The cross and resurrection of Christ and Pentecost are reconciliatory events – the main theme in the whole of the Bible. Both Jesus and the Holy Spirit have been sent to undo the effects of Adam's sin (Genesis 3:5,23) that separated God from mankind.

In 1 Corinthians 13, Paul placed love as the foundation of all relations. If love is present, then the relationship will develop and function as God does. Love is the first fruit of the Spirit Paul lists in Galatians 5:22. This tells us that if we are to see healthy relationships develop and mature, we need the Holy Spirit as the person to indwell us, and also to lead and guide us. Paul said in Romans 8:9 that those who do not have the Spirit of Christ do not belong to Christ. This means the Spirit of God plays a pivotal role in our relationship with God. Not only does He initiate the reconciliation of sinful man and God, He maintains this key relationship, and within it He empowers the believer to function as God instructs them to and expand the Kingdom of God.

The image on the cover of this book is of a bridegroom and his bride. It can also be seen as a man charged with a task to fulfil and the helper he has been given. In Genesis 2:17, God gave Adam a job to do. Interestingly, in verse 18, God gives Adam a helper to walk next to him. This helper was not there to do his work for him, but to assist Adam so he was not totally self-reliant in completing his given tasks.

The word 'Helper' is seen in Isaiah 41 where God describes Himself as Israel's "Helper". Isaiah 40:31 ends with those who wait upon the Lord shall renew their strength and Isaiah 41:1 begins with the same saying of renewing strength and being a comfort to God's people. God called Israel to a specific task; to be light to the Gentiles (Isaiah 42:6; Isaiah 49:6; Isaiah 52:10; Isaiah 60:3; John 8:12; Acts 13:47; Acts 26:23) and God said He would be Israel's Helper to comfort, empower, guide and teach them. In the New Testament, Jesus said He would send the Helper to come to His disciples after He left (John 14:16). The word helper in Greek is *parakletos* which means someone who walks at our side to help us. The Spirit of God, our Helper, indwells us to help us live within our relationships with Him and others in the way God wants us to live. Like a good wife is to her husband (Proverbs 18:22), the Spirit of God helps us depend on Him to complete our task. It is the Spirit who helps us undergo total makeover, a metamorphoses, like a caterpillar that emerges from a cocoon as a beautiful butterfly.

The devil will do all he can to keep us from realising how desperately we need the fellowship of God. He will expend all he has to trick, lie, camouflage, deceive and even kill to stop us from truly knowing God and the fulfilment this relationship brings. He knows it is an eternal relationship. He will employ all he has access to, which are non-eternal things, to blind and distract us from finding the reason for which we were created. This reason is to walk with and worship God in true love and unity. There is no greater purpose, no better reason and fulfilment in the life of any human being – whether earthly or eternal.

The risk of losing what we have

If a man who is approaching the last phase of his life writes a book, it would be about what he deems most important. The apostles, together with the other believers, expected to see Jesus returning while they were still alive. In their minds His return was imminent and so they encouraged all believers to remain "in Him" – remain close to Jesus. In 1 John, John goes to great lengths to talk about God's love, how to understand it, how to respond to it, and how to remain in it, particularly in 1 John 2:18-29. John warns us that we should not allow the world to get between God and us, and he refers to many antichrists. This means there will be many ways that the deceiver will try to harm the relationship we have with God. In verses 22-23, he says that our relationship with the Father is dependent on our relationship with the Son. John says the key aspect the enemy will challenge is Jesus Christ being the way to the Father. If he succeeds in breaking your relationship with Christ, he has destroyed your relationship with the Father as well. We need to ensure that the truth remains in us. How can the truth then be stolen from us? It is when we doubt who Jesus is and what He has done. This way we run the risk of losing what we have. John devoted this letter to telling us that the relationship we have with Christ and the Father is and should be our main focus. Not surprisingly, it is also the main focus of the enemy.

In 1 John 3, John continues by saying Jesus came to destroy the devil's work. What then is the devil's work? In Matthew 1:21 we see that the devil's work is to spread sin in people's lives. The broader definition of sin is 'separation' and we see this clearly in Genesis 3 that details man's fall from grace. Sin separates mankind from eternal life, from God's presence and from one another, and sin causes the first and second death. In the context of relationships, separation means either preventing relating to God or the slow destruction of an existing relationship with God.

It is not the goal of this book to fully explain sin, but it is worth considering what sin does to our relationship with God and each other. In short, from the account in Genesis 3, Adam and Eve sinned. When Adam and Eve sinned; they ran from God and hid; fear gripped them and they became naked (loss of glory). They were banished from God's presence and they lost some of the unique attributes they received from God's image and likeness. Adam denied culpability, he lied and blamed his wife, his son killed his brother, and so it goes. What this reveals is the incredibly destructive effect sin has on all relationships.

Chapter 11

Covid and relationships

I f ever mankind has undergone a test to evaluate what is most important to us as humans, it was the restrictions imposed on us during the Covid pandemic. As Christians, our faith in God who promises to protect us, heal us and provide all we need during trying times was tested, as were our values. What do we value most? In many cases what we say and what we do are not in agreement. Do I value my possessions more, or do I prefer to spend more time, if I am able to, with my family? After all, where I spend most of my time and energy reveal what I value most. This book highlights the eternal value of the relationships we forge with God first and with others second. Our value as individuals, our hope, purpose and future are secure to the extent that we are in a relationship with Christ Jesus. From here all our other relationships take shape.

My aim here is not to express an opinion regarding the nature, origin or cause of the virus. All I want to do is highlight how the world-crisis relates to the theme of the book. Across the world, societies were under strict lockdown, and all of society was affected in one way or another.

Many families were cut off from their loved ones. Some of the positives that came out of the enforced separation was that we began to realise how much we missed meeting with others – and how much we enjoyed the enforced time spent with family members. We stopped and considered what was important.

Some of the negatives were the trillions of dollars wiped off balance sheets and the thousands of families who lost loved ones to the disease and were not able to adequately bid farewell to those who passed away. Reports of domestic violence and divorce soared, highlighting that while families were locked in their homes together, it did not mean their relationships were in a healthy state. But the lockdowns also gave us the opportunity to recognise that God's ultimate intention for us is to live with Him and each other.

Over the past century we, as humanity, created greater distances between ourselves, which is a reflection of the distance we have created between ourselves and God. We were never created to be apart from God, nor from each other. Eternity awaits us where we will be together forever.

Count the cost

Not all relationships have the same importance. In Luke 14:25-35, Jesus says He should be number one in our lives, and that we should count our own lives second to His. What we lose for His sake we will receive, plus a reward. In this passage He warns that what is dearest and closest to us could get in our way of following Him. We should become what Paul describes in Romans 12:1 as "living sacrifices". If we conclude that following God is worth it all, then we should also conclude that no cost is too high to follow Him. We should set priorities for ourselves when we allocate time to the things we have to do. Jesus stated that a relationship with Him should be held at the highest level. He even says we are to forsake all others if we are committed to follow Him. Abraham had to leave his father's house as a sign of obedience. Jesus' disciples had to leave their family businesses to obey His call. Choosing to enter a relationship with Jesus will be a costly journey. Giving Him centre stage in our lives will cost us other relationships (Matthew 10:34-38 and Luke 12:51-53). However, not putting Jesus first in our relationships will cost us dearly. We ought to take our cue from the men of old who chose to believe God and followed Him into glory; they didn't look back, nor turn back. They set their sights on the eternal city of God.

The sands of time

In Ecclesiastes, Solomon points out that days and seasons come and go – our interests change as we grow older and there is a time for everything. Solomon tells us that all things begin and end with God. In Ecclesiastes 3:11 Solomon says God has transcended the seasons and events of this world by placing eternity in the heart of man. The word "eternity" here, when translated from Hebrew, means, "a hidden or unknown duration." This expression denotes man's finite existence; our inability to understand ancient beginnings and distant futures, and our inability to alter these. God has not given man the faculty to comprehend things beyond our existence on earth. Solomon's book is presented as if he himself is the person who set out to understand the world, yet he came to the conclusion that mankind, while on this earth, is finite and so is our understanding. When he says that God has placed eternity in the hearts of men, he is saying God has placed a longing for significance in mankind that reaches beyond life on earth. Mankind has a yearning to reconnect with his Creator who is timeless.

It is with this backdrop that Solomon writes that everything done without a relationship with God is meaningless, empty and void of fulfilment. A relationship with God is what gives us our sense of what is right and wrong, what pleases Him and what doesn't, what is beneficial and what is not. When we grow in a relationship with God, we begin to see what has value and purpose in this world, and understand what Solomon meant when he said things on earth will come and go – which are things we should not invest too much time in. But Solomon also hints that there are hidden things we need to invest in – the things this world despises – and these begin with placing God first.

If we do so, we return to what God desired for Adam before he lost his intimacy with God. As descendants of Adam, we carry a finite and limited existence yet we have been given a longing to go beyond the time and space this world offers and investigate the things of God – the things He allows us to see while we toil on earth. If we are able to, we will find incredible fulfilment and rest as we pursue what is important to Him. These pursuits are investments that follow us into the life to come. In Jesus' own words in Matthew 7:21-23: "Not everyone who says to Me, 'Lord, Lord' shall enter the kingdom of heaven..." show that a relationship with Jesus is what carries us across the great divide between this life and an eternal life with God. Solomon suggested that God has placed a longing in mankind to know Him. However, since the beginning of time, Satan has set his sights on either preventing mankind from knowing God or destroying any relationship mankind has with God.

There are, as Paul says, key aspects we need to take note of. Their effect on the life of every believer is profound. They are hope, faith and love. Our faith, to the extent that we have developed it, allows us to tackle big projects and our drive helps us complete them. Hope, the anchor of our souls, will one day not be needed anymore. Both faith and hope are tools to assist us in sculpting our relationship with God. Once all our work on earth is done, what will be left are the very things we have spent our time on.

We will do well to structure and develop our routines, activities and personal likes in such a way that they allow us to sculpt the correct image. Our individual lives are like a river that needs banks as boundaries to shape and direct our paths. What flows with us is life-giving water that, without boundaries, could dissipate into the dry sand of this world– like many lives have to date. Parents are guardians over their children's lives to teach them how to construct these boundaries for themselves.

Am I a Thomas or a Philip?

John 13 and 14 detail several aspects regarding love. Here we read of an encounter between Jesus and his disciples. Jesus addresses them as "children" and speaks of going somewhere where the disciples cannot yet go. This announcement sparks fear and uncertainty in them. He also gives them a new commandment, which is to love one another. Jesus makes it clear that their love for one another will be a testimony of their discipleship. Jesus foretells Peter's denial of his relationship with Jesus before the rooster crows a third time. After saying this, Jesus then, in John 14:1 makes a remarkable statement: "Do not let your hearts be troubled..." Jesus is relying heavily on the relationship He has spent the last three years building with His disciples. We see this clearly spelt out in John 13:1, which says Jesus loved His disciples to the end. It's not easy to calm people's fears after you have walked with them for several years and you now announce your imminent departure. Only a strong relationship can keep people from losing all hope when their future seems uncertain.

John 14:1 continues Jesus' statement: "...Believe in God, believe also in Me." He was referring to their Jewish ancestors who believed and trusted God for many generations. The word "believe" here means to have a deep trust in someone, and to entrust all you have on that person – there is no 'Plan B'. In John 14:6, Jesus says He is the truth, the way, the life, and the only way to the Father, and in the next verse, he continues with an interesting interchanging of the words "believe" and "know". His disciples needed to understand that knowing Him was to trust Him.

It is at this point that Thomas, who later became known as 'Doubting Thomas', expressed his uncertainty about what lay ahead for all of them. Jesus went straight for the issue in Thomas's heart, namely his lack of trust in Jesus. In Jesus' exchange with Thomas, Jesus used the phrase "know Me" which means the same as "trust Me." Thomas was given a quick lesson on how to allay fears and uncertainty. The answer is to trust Jesus – to take Him at His Word. This is a key issue that emanates from the Old Testament and God's expectation of Israel. He wanted His people to put their trust in Him. He was their source of life, joy, peace and fulfilment. Sadly, they failed to trust God, which caused their death in the Wilderness.

In John 14 we see Thomas expressing the same doubtful heart as the Israelites in the Old Testament. Jesus had said He is going to prepare a place for them, a Promised Land, as God promised

Israel. Jesus was saying that God promised and delivered – they must now also trust Him to promise and deliver. Why can He make such a claim? He's saying that He is God – the same God who led Israel from Egyptian slavery to the Promised Land. Jesus wants them to trust Him and to value Him above all else. Jesus said He was preparing a place for them beyond the curtain of death. This in itself requires deep trust because in death you are helplessly dependent on someone to carry you to the new life. This was Jesus' statement to them. He would make sure they would be with Him after death if they trusted in His provision. All statements Jesus made were meant to ring bells of remembrance of their ancestors' journey to the Promised Land.

Jesus had not finished giving Thomas a lecture in trust when Philip expressed the same doubt. He said he will believe Jesus if Jesus could show Him the Father. Jesus gave Philip the same answer He gave Thomas. He asked Philip, "You still do not know Me?" He goes straight to the key aspect in Philip's heart which is 'unbelief'. They have walked with, touched, heard and seen Jesus the Messiah do mighty miracles, yet both Thomas and Philip failed to trust Jesus and what He was going to do for them.

What follows in John 14:15-30 are the most amazing words as Jesus explains to His disciples what God's relational plan entails. He says that after His departure, the Spirit of God will indwell them. Let us not miss this point. Jesus is saying that God Himself will come and make His home in the body of every believer. Can a human being think of a closer, more intimate and profound relationship than this?

We sometimes miss an important aspect of what Jesus was referring to here. In John 14:11-13 Jesus says He is in the Father and the Father is in Him. He spells out what a perfect relationship should look like, and He goes further by linking works to the relationship. He says the works He does are done by the Father through Him. Imagine Jesus as God walking in the flesh on earth. He could have done so many things, yet He limited Himself to what the Father wanted. His perfect relationship with the Father directed His works. It seems as if Jesus is saying that the closer our relationship with God, the more inclined our ears would be to what the Father wants to do. I dare say if we could hear God better when He speaks to us, we would be less busy with other things. Paul explains this in Ephesians 2:10 when he says that salvation is not achieved by good works, but that it produces good works.

In the John 14 passage, we see how Jesus expressed His concern to both Thomas and Philip for their lack of trust in Him. Jesus uses interchanging words to direct them to the relationship He has been eager to build with each of them. He uses words such as trust, obedience and love to express His relational intentions with them. He even uses the inverse of trust, namely: "Do not let your hearts be troubled," to cut deep into their hearts. He knew that when He left, they would need to grow deeper in the trust He had established with them. Their trust would be their compass, their solid foundation, and would guide them through the threat of death and beyond death.

This trust would be their lifeline to God. Jesus knew that a person's heart is the centre of their personality and is where fear and hopelessness take root. His aim was to develop a relationship-bridge of trust. He knew that it is easy to walk with someone you can touch and feel, and that their trust would be severely tested when the person they walked with was not physically there anymore. When that happens, trusting is not so easy – especially for the disciples who had spent the past three years with Jesus, and it also applies to us today. If we place our trust in the Father, in His Son Jesus and in His Holy Spirit, our hearts will be comforted, encouraged and strengthened.

My expectation

Having knowledge about a person like Nelson Mandela is not the same as having met Nelson Mandela in person. Taking this further; having met a person once is not the same as spending time with that person and getting to know them. Until we have spent time with a person, our preconceived ideas and assumptions are mere fiction. They remain untested perceptions created by us for ourselves from various subjective sources. These perceptions could be wrong. Expectations are birthed from perceptions and are ideas we harbour from the moment we meet a person, and these perceptions will be tested over time.

Our perceptions can be a stumbling block when it comes to knowing God. Many people, in either ignorance or arrogance, harbour wrong perceptions about a loving God who sent His Son to die for His enemies. These wrong perceptions give rise to unreasonable expectations that stop people from developing a relationship with God. Expectations, founded or unfounded, can have a direct impact on the level of trust I place in God. Relationships suffer daily because of unfounded expectations, which can prevent relationships from deepening. In many cases, suspicion prevents either party from truly benefiting from the relationship.

To ascertain if we truly know a person, we can apply the following test: ask yourself what kind of an emotion is evoked in you when you knock on their door late at night. Are you sure they will open and help you with whatever you need, or is it anxiety – as if you were knocking on the door of someone you don't know?

Unfortunately, this is the reality for many believers when it comes to approaching God in their time of need. They might have studied Scripture to some extent and even met Jesus once upon a time at conversion. Yet, the sad reality of their lives is that they live distant from Jesus, and His door is only visited when trouble looms.

God gave us sixty-six books to read, which contain more details about Him than any other single book or collection of writings available to mankind. These books repeat over and over again how much God loves us and desires us to truly know Him personally. He has taken the first step towards us and He initiated the process to reconcile us unto Himself. He has given us His Word to study so that we know what to expect when we approach Him. Not only does His Word tell us what we can expect from God, but it also teaches us what God expects from us. His Word is both the lamp for our feet while we journey here on this earth and it is the key to the door that unlocks eternity with God. God's Word is available to us daily for us to study and ensure we do not create unsubstantiated perceptions and expectations about God and entrance into heaven. Eternal fellowship in God's presence has a high price while on earth, but it is worth giving up all we have, aspire to be, and what this world offers.

The life of the apostle Paul

Since the dawn of humanity, people have made predictions about the future. Some people's predictions were fulfilled and some not. However, when Jesus stands up and makes a prediction, all of humanity should pay attention because Jesus does not speak on His own behalf, but on behalf of the Father.

One such instance is where Jesus makes a prediction in John 16:1-3 about a time coming when those who believe in Him will be killed for their faith. He said that those doing the persecuting will think they are offering service to God. Jesus said of the people who persecute believers, "They have not known the Father nor Me." He was speaking about a time when men like Saul would rise up and drag believers from their homes and throw them into jails. The time Jesus predicted arrived and severe persecution broke out against Christians. In Acts 8, Saul, the Pharisee, spearheading the persecution, brought about a terrible time for all believers and many were scattered throughout the provinces.

The reason I mention Saul is to show how dangerous it can be if we attempt to know the love of God through legalism and not through a relationship. Saul assumed he was offering a service to God, but he was actually fighting God Himself (Acts 9:4). This all changed when Jesus stopped Saul in his tracks. Jesus pursued Saul in order to build a relationship with him. Through this relationship, Jesus would be building relationships with a multitude of churches from that point onwards.

What is needed is a relationship with the author of the Law, not with the cold Law itself as Saul did. The person of Jesus showed Saul grace and truth that changed his legalistic heart to a heart of love. Later on Saul became known as "the apostle of grace". What Saul missed was the love with which God gave the Law in Exodus 20:1-2. When he met Jesus on the road to Damascus, his life changed. He met the person of Jesus – the author and the fulfilment of the Law. At the moment of his conversion, Saul understood that people cannot have a relationship with God based on the Law. The Law is a tutor, not a person. Instead of reconciling people to God, Saul was separating believers and himself from God using the Law. Having met the Lord of love,

Saul's name was changed to Paul. Jesus demonstrated His grace towards Paul and forgave him his ignorance. Paul, who then qualified to be an apostle, became the ambassador of reconciliation. His legalistic obsessive observation of the Law was replaced with a love and grace that could only be found in a relationship with Jesus.

In 2 Corinthians 5:18-19, we see how Paul expresses God's plan of reconciliation as His main purpose in this world. God has begun rebuilding the broken relationship between Him and mankind through Christ. Immediately after Paul said this, in verse 18, he says all believers have also been given this message of reconciliation. This means that God's main purpose in sending Jesus is to restore our relationship with Him.

The calling of Paul to apostleship is a sign of God's grace and love. Paul ignorantly pursued Christians in service of God – so he thought. He ravaged the church and destroyed many relationships. When he met Jesus, he became the ambassador of God in heaven's plan to restore people back to God and each other. It is only the touch of Jesus that changes people deep in their hearts. The only way true love can be born in us and the only way we can respond in love to God love is through a relationship with Jesus. No rules or commands can achieve this.

Troubleshooting

During the Covid pandemic, some of the vaccines used a two-jab vaccination process, while others required only a single dose. Problems developed within several months of the vaccines being administered, whereby, blood clots were found in several patients who had been vaccinated. Because of the blood clots, miscommunication and related risks that were reported, some vaccines were halted and replaced by others. This change caused uncertainty, and unfortunately, some patients who received the first jab, didn't go back for the second.

Not receiving the full required dosage of the vaccine meant the patient was not fully protected against the virus. Patients were hesitant about the second jab for fear of unknown risks. Many opinions were expressed on social networks and media outlets, and because of social media and media, many hopefuls became doubtful about the vaccines.

This example is a clear picture of the process of our salvation. It has been said many times that God did not save us just to ensure our protection against eternal condemnation. God's plan throughout Scripture is to restore man's eternal fellowship with God (2 Corinthians 5:18). The purpose of our salvation is the restoration of fellowship with God, not mere 'fire insurance'. Similar to vaccines that prevent deadly viruses, the Gospel, if I may say, is God's vaccine against the wages of sin. Sin brings death (Genesis 2:17; Romans 6:23) and Jesus Himself came to die as the sacrificial Lamb of God to take away the sins of the world (Matthew 1:21; John 1:29).

Not understanding the process of salvation is like a person receiving only the first jab of the vaccine and not the second, which potentially puts not only their own lives, but those of others in danger. The vaccine has been designed to be administered twice. The first established a beachhead to fight the enemy, and the second to boost the first.

Why then do some people who have received the first jab fall back into sin? It is because they have not received the full treatment prescribed by the vaccine. For a person who has confessed their sins as a sign of true repentance, they have received the first

'Gospel jab'. But to receive full assurance (2 Corinthians 1:22) and the power to live a new victorious life, the second step of the empowering of the Holy Spirit is needed (Acts 1:8; Ephesians 3:16).

When the Spirit of God tugs at the heart of the believer to know God better, it is because God wants the believer to step into the next phase of their salvation. Step one was justification – to be declared righteous before God, but this does not bring true fellowship with the Father. We see this when a child is born. The parent of the child is not only involved in the procreation of the child, but they also ought to be directly involved in the child's upbringing.

The next step in the process is where the believer learns to walk with God. This is similar to the development of a relationship in the lives of a newly married couple. The spouses have to say goodbye to their old single lives and friendships and begin to cling to each other (Genesis 2:24). Many things in the life of the believer will begin to compete for the time the believer has available to spend with God, and a 'war' will begin to rage within the heart of the person.

Selfishness and sinfulness have to be resisted to make way for holiness. When we realise that earthly temptations and desires are more important to us than pursuing fellowship with God, we need to troubleshoot our spiritual lives. We need to test and see if we have indeed received both steps – God's gift of justification by grace through faith (Romans 5:1) and the Holy Spirit's power (Acts 1:8) to live the new victorious life Christ has called us to. Have we, as the Covid vaccine prescribes, achieved both steps in the development process of our spiritual walk with God?

Chapter 12

The bridge of trust

No woven rope can be deemed strong nor can it be calibrated until it is tested and certified. Similarly, trust is only real until we test what we trust. Relationships are the best way where trust can be tested. A relationship provides a platform where trust is established and built up, and also where trust is broken. When studying suspension bridges we can see why some of these bridges can be relied on to ferry passengers and cargo across troubled waters for decades. Suspension bridges are held up by strong cables that carry all the weight. They are only as strong as their anchors. When designing these suspension bridges, engineers ensure the suspending cables are anchored into bedrock. When walking across these bridges, we can rest assured that the engineers who designed them have done research to ensure the anchors are solid.

Trust is the strongest anchor in a relationship because once it is established, it is constant. People base their decisions on the trust that has been established, and their relationships reflect a consistency. Because the anchor exists, those people can be relied on and their actions are fairly predictable. You know how they will react and you are assured of their word. Such relationships display a peace, a healthy stability, and joy.

Looking at the construction of the large suspension bridges again, once the carrying cables have been installed, the rest of the structure is added piece by piece, with the cables acting as a platform on which other features depend. Likewise, trust in any relationship is a platform that ensures many other functions can take place.

To see how trust functions as a platform we can study the framework of a marriage. When the ceremonial marriage vows are exchanged by the parties, they make promises to each other, which are the foundation of trust in the relationship. Everything else that is added to the relationship depends on this trust foundation. Trust can be called a primary function, while other things such as planning, daily tasks, finances, careers, marital intimacy, raising children, accumulation of wealth, peace and joy, openness, protection, forgiveness, and so on, all fall within the framework of secondary functions.

Staying with the metaphor of a suspension bridge, it is able to maintain its own load and that of the passengers and cargo ferried across it because of the strong anchors the cables are secured in. Although suspension bridges are built to last for many years, these anchor points require regular checkups. Any corrosion could spell disaster for both the bridge and its cargo. Should the primary trust be eroded and eventually lost in a relationship, all the secondary aspects of a relationship fall away. Many people say, "trust is earned," hinting that a long period is needed for trust to develop in the hearts and minds of the two people involved. In the context of a marriage, both partners are required to make a wilful decision to trust and be trustworthy.

No better example of the relationship between God and mankind is given to us than the relationship between God and Abraham. When God asked him to sacrifice his son Isaac, he was called to stand alone before God in the 'Audience of One'. His trust in God was tested to its very foundation. Once confirmed as trustworthy, the trust between God and Abraham was a primary trust that allowed many other aspects to be ferried across the platform. The nation of Israel was one of the secondary functions that was made possible by the primary function of Abraham's and God's trust in each other. Abraham's life and legacy provided a platform for Joseph to forgive his brothers for selling him into slavery. The choice Joseph made to forgive his brothers is a formula that touches our lives today. Abraham's legacy also secured the Promised Land for the people of Israel. Through Abraham's salvific faith-model, every believer today can receive God's blessing of the Holy Spirit, which shows the impact a trust-based relationship can have.

God does not lie to us, therefore His Word can be relied on. Having God as a relational partner ensures our lives of consistency, peace, joy and reliability. Unlike humans, God is always faithful. The world can never provide the same sense of security God gives. He is unchangeable, always faithful and trustworthy. To us living in a world where trust seems hard to find, God is our solid anchor and our reliable constant. He is our rock that cannot be moved by any storm or uncertainty; He is not swayed by ever-changing ideologies or worldviews. As a ship's captain relies on his compass to reach his destination, mankind desperately needs God's consistency. Mankind, in our frail existence, cannot rely on human promises that are made and broken every day. We need the trustworthiness and unchangeable character of God to guide us, and provide a safe place for our existence, growth and our development.

A worthwhile goal

In Romans 12:9-21, Paul wrote a passage that is similar to Jesus' Sermon on the Mount in Matthew 5-7. In the NIV Bible, it is titled, 'Love in action'. Paul establishes love as the key value of any relationship. It starts with us. We are to live it out in a way that our actions touch those close to us. In verse 18, he exhorts us to take the lead in promoting love and peace with everyone. In saying, "as far as it depends on you," Paul emphasises that we are to do all we can to maintain all relationships.

When we look at our world and all the distractions enticing our flesh, we find that many things are designed to drive us apart. Our sinful nature pursues wealth, position, ambition and selfishness, which cause us to fall prey to the world's systems that drive a wedge between us. We imagine and expect possessions and promi-nence to bring fulfilment, when fulfilment, rest and peace are only found when our relationship with God and our fellow people are growing and maturing. Relationships are a goal worth pursuing far more than position, prominence, possessions and power. To achieve these worldly pursuits, relationships, which are a key value in God's Kingdom, often are shipwrecked. As we mature in age and wisdom, we will find that relationships carry an inherent value, which material possessions do not have.

Why the silence?

Have you ever felt, when you pray to God, particularly at a time when you need an answer to your next step, that God seems distant? Why does He appear silent when we need His help? There are a few reasons why God sometimes does not answer our prayers. He does not react or respond based on how we think He should. God Almighty did not enter a relationship with us to be dictated to. He remains the benefactor and we the beneficiaries.

There is also a big difference between our needs and our wants. Jesus said in Matthew 6 that the Father knows what we need. These needs flow out of life's basic principles, which are mostly connected to our humanity as God created us. On the other hand, our wants stem our fallen nature from Genesis 3, driven by our sinful desires and unwise decisions.

In Matthew 6 Jesus speaks about our Father in heaven meeting our needs. Jesus makes an effort to refer to the relationship we should be developing with our "Father in heaven". In verses 31-32, Jesus speaks about our needs, which He calls "things". He contrasts the "things" we value and think we need to the right-eousness of God that we critically need. This righteousness from God is Jesus Himself. Through faith in Jesus, we gain a right-standing with God, which is God's righteousness made available to everyone who believes in Him. We are to pursue and seek this right-standing with God more than we pursue and seek other things. Jesus places the relationship with our Father God as the primary focus, and the things we need as secondary. He says the primary will ensure the secondary. However, when it comes to trusting our heavenly Father for this, we seem to fall short.

Needs are met within the context of a relationship between a father and his children. Perhaps we have been asking God to meet our needs, but not invested in making Him Our Father in heaven. With reference to Israel's journey, God met the needs of His people. He was the provider and protector of His people, His called-out ones, not to other nations. Sadly though, adults decide whether or not to build a relationship with God. In many cases believers run to God if and when He supplies their needs. Because of the lack of a relationship with God, people decide to go it alone. This is the one big mistake Israel made in their journey from Egyptian slavery through the Wilderness towards the Promised Land. They did not trust God enough to bring them to their destiny. Instead, they tried to do it by themselves (Deuteronomy 1:29-36). This was a total breakdown in trust and God punished them severely for it.

It is also not uncommon to see our needs not met when and how we expect them to be. We either present our emotionally charged wants camouflaged as needs before God, or we expect God to meet our needs outside the context of a Father-child relationship. In this I want to highlight another aspect that prevents us from receiving an answer from God when we pray. It happens when we make our requests known to God in prayer, when these very requests are already dealt with in Scripture. God will never contradict His own Word and therefore will always provide an answer in line with His Word.

Here's a valuable example. In James 4 the author deals with practical aspects, and in verses 13-17, James says many people make decisions based on their own wisdom. They fail to consult God, and then later they suffer loss. James specifically deals with people relocating to other towns in order to increase their wealth. Many people, when deciding to relocate to increase their wealth, spent time in prayer and later profess they heard God on their decision. It is easier to hear what you want to hear rather than an answer that questions your decision. In the case of relocating, God might appear silent for the reason that His Spirit has already addressed the request in Scripture.

When God seems distant

Any relationship goes through seasons of founding, then growth, times of dryness, sudden challenges, and prevailing uncertainties. As previously said, no relationship grows by itself. Time and seasons are about the only aspects that keep moving without any required human intervention. Most other aspects in life are affected by relationships, and these require constant work if they are to mature.

What if God appears to be silent and distant? Is it because of our sin, or is it perhaps that we do not hear Him speak? When we see how God dealt with the nation of Israel towards the end of the Old Testament, we see a period of 400 years in which God did not speak. Although the Israelites had God's Laws and Commandments, meaning the Moral, Civil and Ceremonial Laws He gave through Moses, there was no direct communication from God. Why would God withdraw and keep His distance if He is such a loving relational God?

I will use an illustration from my own household. I ask my daughter to give my son a message asking him to do something for me. If, a while later he has not done it, I have to ask myself what a father is supposed to do in such an instance. What I would do is call him and repeat my instruction. If he still delays, perhaps because of a distraction and he forgets what I asked him to do, it calls for an intervention on my part. This could be my silence or corrective training given to my son. It could also be that I choose to let my son be for a while to see what his attitude is towards me, his father. When I eventually respond to correct the situation, neither my love for my son, nor my instruction to him has changed. All that is needed is for my son to respond in obedience and fulfil my request. What I am saying is that love is always present, even during times of correction or silence. It is us, in the image of the son, who need to respond and be obedient to the Father's request.

God has given us both the Old and New Testaments. The Old prepares us for the New and the New validates the Old. We have the Old Testament to reveal how God's voice became silent after many years of calling His people back to Himself. It does not mean His love for them changed in any way. His method of calling His people changed to show who would respond to His call to return to Him. He stopped speaking and sent His Son in person, the very image and representation of the Father. The Father's calling changed. He remained silent in order to attract His people's attention to that fact that God was not speaking. During this time of silence, He prepared the people for His own coming – to speak to them in person.

A situation I had several years ago as a pastor in a local church will describe what happens when a father becomes silent. I befriended a successful businessman who showed a desire to know more about the things of God. I invited him to church, but on every occasion, he had an excuse for not attending. My invitations went out for close on a year and so did his excuses. One morning I became frustrated and in my prayer time I asked the Lord to release me from this man who was full of the usual "I will come next week" excuses. I immediately stopped communication and invites. Two weeks went past and on the Sunday morning of the second week I found him standing at the church door with tears in his eyes. I was elated to see him there. That morning he could not wait for the alter call to respond. He got saved that day. The next morning when I saw him, I asked him what made him come to church. He said: "Every time you invited me, I knew you were praying for me and that I was under your cover before God. I kept living in my same old sinful ways. Every week your message assured me I can postpone for another week. Your messages allowed me to remain in my business, which was a distraction from the voice in me that I knew was God calling me. The day you stopped inviting me, that day I felt as if the whole world changed. I felt as if God had removed His grace and covering over me. Nothing was going to stand in the way of me making sure I met with God."

Also on the subject of God's silence within a relationship, in Luke 17:3-10, Jesus spoke of forgiving each other. When He said we need to keep forgiving a brother unreservedly when he repents for mistakes, His disciples responded by saying, "Increase our faith." Jesus gave his disciples a short but important lesson on when to use faith and when to obey. He told them of a master who expected his servant to wait upon him at the dinner table. Jesus wanted to clear an uncertainty in the disciples' understanding regarding faith and immediate obedience. They were a bit confused. Jesus set their thinking straight by saying that some matters call for immediate obedience and not for prolonged delays while you wait for God to respond to your uncertainty. Jesus said the servants should serve their master and thereafter they could partake of the meal. This parable has a direct bearing on why obedience could have a direct link to God's silence. It might be that we are unsure of our responsibility to obey, like the servant who had to wait on his master.

While we wait for God to respond to our uncertainty, His response might well be no response. Instead of us asking what to do, we should rather act on what we have been given to do. A person who understands their relationship with God does not require another answer from God. If we are still waiting for God to respond to our uncertainties, we need to do some soul searching in case we are doing the same as the disciples in Jesus' parable. God is waiting for our obedience in a particular area. He has already spoken to us through His Word and does not need to speak any louder or repeat Himself. It is us who need to respond in obedience and do what He has said. In this instance our relationship with God is healthy, but we need to distinguish when to wait in anticipatory faith and when to practice immediate obedience. After all, ignorance breeds uncertainties, doubts and delays, while an informed person walks in obedience, which is how we demonstrate our reciprocal love to God.

Stuck in a moment

As pastors, evangelists and teachers, we are quick to preach threatening sermons about hell and eternal condemnation to our listeners, yet we do not always tell them what they are saved into. We tell people how they are to get saved, but we do not inform them what the result of salvation is. Our sermons put forward truth about salvation, but we also need to tell people why eternal damnation is a reality. They must understand that refusing a loving God comes with an irrevocable sentence.

The process of salvation that God instituted was not to make mankind look better on paper, nor was it to wash away mankind's iniquities. At its core, it serves to reconcile mankind into a renewed friendship with God his Creator. From the account in Genesis where God dwelt with His people, all the way through to Revelation, we see God establishing an eternal friendship with all believers in Christ. God's intention was not only to justify sinners through the blood of Jesus; His plan was to sanctify believers by the Spirit and to eventually glorify them. Teachers and pastors need to emphasise that through God's plan of salvation, every believer has the opportunity to become God's personal friend. Refusing this great plan of salvation is not refusing a kind of retirement package God is marketing. Refusing salvation is refusing God Himself. It is refusing a deep friendship or fellowship with the one who created you. Eternity with God is meant for those who are His friends. We can see in Revelation 21-22 how God is building a kingdom.

Friends of God

Throughout this book, a relationship with God has been the focus. We are not saved to merely live a life on this earth and one day die and be taken to heaven. If this was so, then Jesus would not have prayed the prayer He did in John 17:3. His words ring true today: "Now this is eternal life: that they may know you, the only true God." Jesus Himself called us His friends (John 15:15). How are we to evaluate the quality of the friendship we have with God? What indicators are available to us to judge if we are friends of God.

A meaningful relationship, as the Bible describes marriage, requires us to walk away from others and to cling to someone specific. Our attention, focus, affection, dedication and devotion have to be kept for one person only. James uses the context of marriage to describe an adulterous person as someone who promised to be faithful unto death and has been found unfaithful (James 4:4). James calls it adultery when the love that believers promised to God is given to the world by loving the desirable things the world offers. He says to devote yourself to the world and what it offers is to make God your enemy. James allows no choice in his statement. You either love and devote yourself to God or you abandon God and love the world.

How then do we evaluate our relationship with God? When God created Adam and Eve, it was God's intention to have fellowship with mankind (Genesis 1:26). The level of fellowship would not be the same as the fellowship within the Godhead because humans are not divine. God created Adam with a spiritual faculty unlike any other created being. Mankind can relate to God on various levels. God breathed His Spirit into man (Genesis 2:7) and because of this, mankind has a personal link to God no other created being has.

The desire for relations that God put in man is uniquely fulfilled by God alone. Since man's fall, people have unsuccessfully attempted to draw created things to themselves to fulfil this desire for relations. To evaluate the existence and depth of our relationship with God, we need only look around and take stock of what we surround ourselves with. A cluttered life full of worldly things may indicate a person who is still searching for the true loving relationship only God can give. The cycle of hoarding more and more worldly goods increases a person's desperation, because the more they gather, the more they realise material possessions can never take God's place.

By indulging in the niceties the world offers, a wedge is being driven into the relationship between God and us. This wedge is not a battering ram nor a sudden explosion. It is a calculated push by the devil, taking little steps at a time to open a void between us and God. He does this so he can fill it with things that decay, rust and break. As he did when he tempted Jesus in Luke 4, he offers us worldly things that have no eternal value. If we begin to indulge in and lust after what the world offers, we begin to commit spiritual adultery. This means we abandon God and cling to the world. Adultery, as James describes it, is when we know we have promised our devotion to God, but are willing to entertain the world's advances. We are called to be friends of God and an enemy of the world.

If we do not take heed of the devil's plans, we will eventually find ourselves alienated from God. This means we will be shut out from relational intimacy with God. James 4:4 says we make a choice to walk away from God and join ourselves to the world.

Do rules define God?

After God redeemed Israel from Egyptian slavery, He took them to Mount Sinai where He covenanted with His people. This is known as the Old Covenant. After God created and befriended Adam, He gave him a boundary, explained as the permission to eat from one and not the other tree. This boundary was not meant to merely serve as cold 'do and don't' rules. It was a measure to maintain a healthy relationship. The covenant at Mount Sinai was accompanied by many rules, known as the Civil, Ceremonial and Moral Laws, which were meant to make the relationship with God practical. The rules explained to Israel who God is and what He is like. It made Him practical to them as it detailed how they were to understand His holiness. These right-eous laws explained the person of God to the people of God. Connected to these rules or laws was the required obedience to walk in them, and refusing to obey them meant opposing the person of God Himself. An example of this is when the first king of Israel, Saul, abandoned God's laws and the result was that God abandoned him (1 Samuel 15:26).

When Adam and Eve sinned, they not only violated God's commands; they violated His trust, which touched His very person. This is seen daily when trust is broken in intimate rela-tionships by one of the partners. This violation can take years to heal and, in many instances, it cannot be repaired.

Even when Adam sinned, he was still tied to a relationship with God, albeit a strained relationship. God remained Adam's Creator despite Adam's sin.

Putting God first

The essence of the Ten Commandments is to put God first and then our neighbour. The core of these commandments is the maintenance of the relationship between God and mankind. The commandments are not the focus; they are tools to help us under-stand what is important to God. They are there to govern and protect relationships. If this were not so, God would have dealt with us the same way He deals with the earth, sun and moon that He created. He is distant from them and they function based on the boundaries He has assigned to them. Not so with mankind. His desire is to dwell with mankind, to walk with us, to communi-cate with us, and to provide everything we need.

Why is it that we live so far from the relationship God proclaims in His Word? To understand this, we need to understand why God had to come and pay for His enemy's sins. Are we God's enemies? Paul tells us we are in Colossians 1:21. Can an enemy of God be changed into a friend of God? In John 15:15 Jesus says we become the friends of God. The total sacrifice of Christ, beautifully explained by Paul in Philippians 2:1-11, reveals the extent to which God values relationships.

To further understand this, we need to go back to Genesis 3, before sin entered the world. In Genesis 1-2 we see how God intended to be man's friend. God allowed mankind into His creation and God was relationally committed to the man and woman He created. To govern the relationship, God gave them rules, which were the boundaries of life or death as He put it (Genesis 2:16-17). This is a well of truth for us to draw from today. Man was given tasks to perform, but the predominant reason was to fellowship with God.

We see that while Adam was working, God did not treat him as a servant, God also allocated time for Adam to fellowship with his Creator. Work was never the ultimate goal of man's existence. Our modern world with all its complexities and demand is what we have created.

No matter how much we dedicate ourselves to creating material wealth while we live, none of it will follow us into the life hereafter. The only passport or guarantee to entering heaven is, "Do I know you," in the words of Jesus (Matthew 7:21-23). Here Jesus equates a relationship with Himself as doing the will of the Father. 1 John 2:3 says knowing God is obeying His will or His commands. John says something remarkable in verse 5. He says that obedience to God's commands leads to the perfection of our love for God. What then is the will of the Father? It is simple obedience. Putting God first in our lives is therefore not doing many things for Him. It is knowing Him by treating His Word with the respect it deserves. Knowing His Word is knowing His will. Knowing His will enables us to obey Him, which is how we demonstrate our love for Him.

Chapter 13

Solomon – a case study

I f ever there was a man who understood what it meant to walk with God, it was King Solomon. Solomon is known throughout the world for his wisdom and riches; he is not as well known for his time of apostasy. He is the author of three books in the Bible. In his youth he penned the Songs of Solomon; in his middle-age he wrote Proverbs, and in his older years he wrote Ecclesiastes. Both Proverbs and Ecclesiastes are full of wisdom for daily living.

Where Proverbs provides us with wisdom to anticipate and wisely deal with various matters in life, Ecclesiastes invites us to be introspective and set priorities for this life that will affect us in the life to come. These two books, read in tandem, provide a powerful platform to every believer to study and evaluate how one of the most influential men in history walked with God. Was his walk unreproachable? Not at all. Solomon was the wisest man ever, yet he made some big mistakes. In a personal account in Ecclesiastes, Solomon lays bare his highs and lows – his autobiography is there for our instruction. His main theme is that all pursuits in life are empty except fearing God and obeying His Word.

Solomon is a reflection of how true fulfilment is only possible in Jesus. In chapter after chapter, Solomon gives an account of what he found when pursuing different avenues in his quest for fulfilment and joy. We see phrases like, "I said to myself" and "I have seen another evil…" These retrospective comments are made by a man who pursued every possible pleasure in life and still was unable to find fulfilment – apart from God.

We should not lose sight of the fact that Solomon was the king who ruled at the pinnacle of Israel's existence after his father David. Under his leadership Israel possessed the Promised Land; the land of milk and honey. Solomon was the designer and inhabitant of an incredible palace, and he built the most extravagant Jewish temple ever. Despite all his remarkable endeavours, he fell short, by his own admission, of finding true meaning and purpose in life. Material possessions and human friendships could not fill the gap only God can fill.

Solomon personified the expectation gap. He pursued philosophy, wisdom, knowledge and study, pleasure, laughter, wine and sensuality, creativity, activity, hard work, building projects, cultivation, wealth and possessions, livestock, concubines, ambition, advancement, prestige, morality and even religion, just to prove them all to be empty pursuits. His expectations were dashed when compared to the reality of a meaningless life without God.

In terms of possessions, Solomon had it all. He exemplified divine and profound wisdom, and he met with God face-to-face on more than one occasion. We have to ask how a man so gifted, so rich, so close to God, could reach a place where he broke fellowship with God. From the beginning of Ecclesiastes, we see his powerful claim that all of life is meaningless, empty and worthless. His rhetoric gives a sense of hopelessness and despair. Solomon uses the statement, "under the sun," more than twenty times throughout his book, referring to all things done in man's wisdom and strength. The phrase gives the impression of mankind who has walked away from God in their attempt to find the illusive fulfilment and happiness.

Jesus, in His parable of the Lost Son, tells a similar story. The son was with his father. He rebelled and pursued a life that seemed better to the one he had. He broke fellowship with his father, but when he came to his senses, he returned to his father.

Scripture tells us that God is the centre of all life and purpose, yet mankind falls victim to the next best gimmick advertised. Dream after dream; purchase after purchase; project after project, mankind, like Solomon, slips away from God as we take our eyes off the person of God and believe that the world has something better to offer than the friendship of God. Solomon found out that what is new today is old tomorrow; a desire fulfilled leads to a greater desire. As knowledge increases so does confusion and wealth, like a millstone of worry around the neck. It is unimaginable how painful and bitter life must be at the end when the realisation sets in that time cannot be replaced. It is impossible to retrace the steps of foolish worldly pursuits in order to develop a relationship with our Creator.

In his old age, Solomon laments the time he wasted in the pursuit of empty dreams, mirages, and the bitter regrets when expectations of fulfilment bring disappointments. He urges every reader to stop and reflect; to take stock of what they keep themselves busy with. Throughout his book, Solomon builds the argument that without God, all the pursuits of mankind are empty and utterly disappointing, and this disappointment will be experienced in this life and the life hereafter. Solomon concludes by contrasting the life of a person without God to the life of a person who walks in fellowship with God. Similar to the lost son, Solomon has felt the pain of a life without God. The conclusion to Solomon's argument is that mankind has to go beyond "under the sun". He has to return to his friendship with God. This is where true fulfilment and purpose are found.

Solomon's biography is a case study that suspends all other arguments and ideologies. No one can rival his fame, wealth, wisdom, politics and administration; no one knows better than Solomon how to dream about, plan and build a palace fit for a king. The scale and perfection of his achievements remain legendary. Despite all he had, all he did, and all he knew, he concludes that a relationship with God far outweighs all this world can offer, and that nothing in this world can satisfy the insatiable longing in mankind to be relationally connected to his Creator. As a practical test, we can evaluate our own worldly pursuits and those of powerful people today to see how much or how little God features in these pursuits.

Unfinished business

Every time I have to attend or host a funeral as a pastor, I am touched by the pain of those left behind after the passing of a loved one. Beyond the pain experienced at a funeral, I have observed another pain that people experience. This is the pain of 'unfinished business' that is created when relationships are allowed to deteriorate, and in many cases suffer complete shipwreck.

Relationships can be very difficult to maintain, especially the ones close to you, because they are in your personal space, much like your shadow from which you cannot run. They require great sacrifice and the investment of time to just survive stormy seasons.

God in His wisdom did not make mankind a master of time; God kept the keys to time safely stored away. In Ecclesiastes 3, Solomon tells us that time is a commodity that governs our lives. Mankind will never become the master of time. Despite our best efforts to remain forever young and reverse the ageing process, time remains out of our grasp. If not used wisely, time will cause many to suffer as they live with constant regret over things they never did; words said in haste; visits that never took place because the business of life prevented them from spending quality time with loved ones. This deep regret turns into pain, which can be compared to the pain suffered at the loss of a loved one.

Part Four

Making every effort

Chapter 14

The lost years

As a pastor, I have heard the phrase, "If only I..." too many times. Parents who spent most of their time building careers and not investing in their relationships with their children are the predominant candidates for the "If only I..." statements. Once the time for making relational investments is over, no amount of money can recover the lost years. What parents are left with after years raising their children, is a reflection of how well they managed their time with their children. Many elderly people are abandoned in old-age homes, and we can only wonder why the children do not see a need to visit their parents. In many cases, elderly people in these homes die from loneliness rather than from health-related issues. Their hearts are weak from the regret of not establishing a relationship with their children when they had the time to.

This book aims to highlight the importance and value of relationships. Unfortunately, because we are slow learners, we allow this broken world to destroy our relationships. In many cases, relationships are like clean water poured into a muddy bucket. The water represents our relationships, and the bucket represents this broken world. Although God is not to blame for the brokenness in this world, He does offer us the wisdom to manage our relationships in this perverse world. Unfortunately, we procrastinate; we postpone work on our relationships in order to satisfy self. We are the most important thing to ourselves and also the most destructive.

The aspect of 'unfinished business' can be a painful experience, serving as a constant reminder to us that time has passed and will never be recovered. The realisation sets in that we could have spent it better. This is especially true when we have foolishly and selfishly neglected our loved ones.

The battle for our spirits

God does not want our spirits to be consumed by the god of this world – the devil. God wants a relationship with our human spirit so that He can instil His will within us. If this good relationship is established, He will guide us to a good and peaceful life. However, the devil is active too. He wants to get hold of our human spirit to influence us to do his will. He has come to destroy us and he speaks to our 'flesh' – our indwelling sin and earthly lusts that we inherited from our forefathers (1 Peter 1:18). Here there is a battle between two forces, and in this battle, God is a jealous God. He wants us to be zealous with His zeal in this battle.

Above all

The title of this book speaks of a relationship that is worth pursuing above all others. A relationship with the living God is a destiny that every life lived on earth ought to pursue. A relationship with the almighty God is worth it all. He is worth giving up our all, and surrendering everything we have set our hopes and dreams on. He is before all things and above all power (John 3:31). He is more fulfilling than all the wealth, prestige and position this world can offer. We are to forsake all others to cling to Him. It does not mean we abandon all other relationships; it simply means we give God the pre-eminence in all our affiliations. 'God first' is a motto that truly expresses how we view God's place in our lives.

Throughout this book I have focused on one of God's key attributes. Father, Son and Holy Spirit are always seen as relational beings and act in this fashion, whether in heaven or on earth. The Trinity exemplifies a decision-making platform that reveals a unity within the plurality of persons. This unity is expected where God is present. It is therefore expected that if the church is the bride, betrothed to Jesus, that she would be a body that exemplifies unity. If she is to be, what Scripture portrays as Jesus' judicial equal, then she should be a church who has a deep understanding of unity.

Love and unity are embodied in Christ's incarnation and His sacrifice for a people who have fallen out of unity with God. Placing God at the centre of our lives will ultimately shape our relationship with Him and with those around us.

In 1 John 3:1-2, John says that by means of God's love, we should be called "children" of God. Here again we see how love expresses itself within the realm of a relationship. If the Father of the children express love towards the children, is it not then correct to expect the children to show love to each other? In Colossians 3:11-43, Paul says that because Christ is over all and in all, we are to clothe ourselves with Him. This way we will begin to embody His nature, which is love. Him in us will develop a focus in our lives whereby we value relationships. As His nature starts to dictate our actions, we begin to do what Pauls urges us to do; we will pursue peace to be one body living in peace. By looking at what Paul urges us to pursue, it becomes clear that his focus is healthy thriving relationships between those who are members of the body of Christ. To be a member of the body of Christ, we need to pursue love, forgiveness, humility and gentleness – all of which are the fruit of the Spirit of fellowship found in Galatians 5:22-23.

In Ephesians 4:3, Paul urges us to "make every effort" to maintain unity.

Opposing forces

The Bible speaks about these opposing spiritual forces: the Holy Spirit vs. the spirit of the antichrist. Within the Holy Spirit is the good and acceptable and perfect will of God (Romans 12:2), and in the spirit of antichrist is the influence of the devil to exalt ourselves and exclude God and His will. In this battle, God is zealous for us and provides us with this zeal as a driving force, an enthusiasm, to attain God's goal for us, so that we overcome the spirit of antichrist. This means that our human spirit turns away from being directed towards the world. In other words, instead of only being occupied with our own interests and needs and the things of this world, we are turned towards heaven and become united with God's will, which is good, perfect, and eternal.

While working with us, God is zealous and He uses all the means at His disposal to instil His zeal in us through the ups and downs of life. He sends us circumstances that will show us the sin dwelling within us, and He gives us power and zeal to overcome the sin that wants to destroy our joy and peace in God.

God's zeal versus human zeal

There is a difference between God's zeal and human zeal. God's zeal has a future and a hope, but the driving force of human zeal is only about one's own life, interests, and earthly advantages. God's zeal drives us to a new life where we are willing to give up our self-life to find the life that is in Christ Jesus – eternal life.

This zeal leads us to the death of Christ – where we can put to death the sin that dwells in us, and be made alive in our human spirit for eternal life (2 Corinthians 4:6-18). The portion of our human spirit that is made alive becomes our light and radiance eternally.

God's desire is for all people to enter into this space by being delivered from the clutches of sin and partaking in a victorious life (Romans 6:22). "But now having been set free from sin, and having become slaves of God, you have your fruit to holiness, and the end, everlasting life."

God is jealous for our spirits – and He gives the necessary grace for us to succeed.

Throughout history there have been many fearless people who embarked on great exploits, but not all exploits have left a positive impact and a legacy worth celebrating. Humanity needs people of courage and vigour to push the boundaries; individuals who dare to break out and establish beachfronts for others to follow.

Many of the great accomplishments throughout ancient and modern history are done in the name of God. Let us imagine for a minute that God did not know that His name was attached to these exploits. Do you think He would agree to His name being used? Perhaps He would be alarmed to hear He was involved in some of the exploits? It is one thing to label your exploit as God-ordained, and it is another to ask and wait for His approval. I want to say at this point that my focus is more on the exploits of believers when ignorance, pride, arrogance and blindness are main contributing factors to some of their exploits.

My goal is not to discuss what great exploits really are, but to put forward how they are to be approached. Often we look at men's achievements from a human point of view. It might require mind-blowing brainpower to pull it off, but do we consider God's view and validation of such exploits? When we read Ecclesiastes, we are reminded that some of the greatest exploits under the sun have been viewed as meaningless, empty and worthless. I am not saying we should be pew-warmers and not strive to do anything. My point is that within the context of a relationship with God, we can be guided in such a way that all our exploits centre on His approval, His provision, and His blessing.

Ask Abraham what it was like when he embarked on an exploit and created Ishmael. Once such exploits take place they cannot be halted. Some, created without godly wisdom, do more harm than good. Paul says in 1 Corinthians 3:10-15 that the works of all believers, great and small, will one day be tested by God's fire. All will be revealed and judged based on God's value system – not man's. Sadly, many celebrated exploits are littered with human stamps of approval, but no stamp of approval from God.

What does Scripture reveal to believers who are pioneers and achievers? How do we ensure our exploits carry God's approval? We need to know that what our eyes see, the opportunities in front of us, the budgets, the crowds, the designs, the unexpected wind-fall – all of these could be distractions. Jesus made it clear that the secrets of the Kingdom of God are not found lying around on the streets for everyone to see. It is when we enquire from God that we begin to see His hand in opportunities – the right opportunities. How do we enquire from God? Acts 16:6-10 contains a remarkable portion of Scriptural instruction. It says that Paul and his companions travelled and felt good at entering a certain region to spread the Gospel. It was a noble exploit; it fitted into the framework and vision Jesus shared in Acts 1:8. They were doing the right thing as far as could be seen. Then, Scripture says they were kept from preaching the Word in the area they planned to enter. There are not many other places in the New Testament saying the Holy Spirit stopped someone from preaching. He moved them to another location to preach, which becomes clear in verse 10. During that night Paul had a vison directing him to where God wanted Him to go.

My question to all great pioneers and fearless people is, when last did the Spirit of Jesus (Acts 16:7) stop you from embarking on a project or journey? Perhaps what would help us in our planning and enquiring of God before we start is to see the future where all our works will be tested (1 Corinthians 3:10-15). What I would like to highlight here is the remarkable discernment Paul and his companions showed when they were "prevented from entering". I have been guilty many times, when I have been "prevented from entering", I have drawn the sword of "perseverance and longsuffering" instead of stopping to hear the voice of the Spirit of Jesus. We are all vulnerable to the powerful wave of ambition that can make us seem great and earn us a great deal of human praise, but we chose a wave that 'beached' us and our journey came to a halt. We chose a wave we did not really have the calling and gifting for, and we were so enamoured with the budget, scale and prominence, that we lost focus of where it was taking us.

Before and during our great exploits, Scripture shows that the Spirit of Jesus can be heard when situations and doors, to our utter frustration, close in our faces. He can be heard in the soft wise and humble voices of trustworthy companions and in His Word, giving us clear direction. Personally, I have found that it is not the first door that opens, but the second or third one I have to enter. It depends on how much trust I give and receive in my personal relationship with the Spirit of Jesus that makes the difference. Going out into the nations we risk it all. We carry a sack full of Gospel seeds, which has the capacity to affect great change in people's lives. But, for us to one day hear, "Well done, good and faithful servant," we need to lay down our all to see Him do it all.

Mankind's desperate urge

When reading Genesis 1-2, we see that God's intention for mankind was to have a close mutual relationship. Throughout the whole of the Old Testament, despite Israel's rebellion and unfaithfulness, God did not waver in His love and commitment to His people. When reading Genesis 1-2 and Revelation 21:3, we are again reminded of God's purpose to co-habit with the people of His pasture. It is clear throughout Scripture that God's intention has always been to exist relationally with mankind.

Mankind was created with the intention of being part of God's family. With such a close connection to God, mankind's identity has been inextricably linked to God our Creator. Even though not every person, today and throughout history, worships God nor acknowledges Him as their Creator, He remains the Father of all of mankind. This Father-child relationship is the essence of mankind's worth, the purpose of our lives on earth, and it is what brings Him joy. Mankind was created by God to fully depend on our Creator. Humanity was never meant to live alone and be independent. God created Adam to be His friend, and He followed the same principle when He created Eve. Mankind has no other purpose for existing apart from God. We are created by God, for God and our whole being depends on our relationship with our heavenly Father. Should we decide to live a life apart from God, we enter a journey on this earth where we have no purpose, no worth or value and no future, whether earthly or eternal. Should God decide to withdraw from this relationship, mankind has no hope and no life. We would have no reason to live.

When people separate themselves from their Creator, or when we deny the undeniable, which is our link with God our Father, we cut ourselves off from the true source of life. The relationship between God and mankind provides us with an identity that we desperately need. It anchors our sense of worth and commands the direction of our labours and exploits on this earth. In the absence of such a relationship, we lose rationality and the ability to relate to God. When mankind sinned in the Garden of Eden (Genesis 3:6), they lost their God-given identity. They did not lose their link to God their Creator, but they lost the fellowship of God. The entrance of sin brought separation between God and man, and mankind died spiritually. This means they were no longer able to abide in God's presence due to their sin. They no longer had the sustaining presence of God they needed to live eternally. In Romans 8:7, Paul describes the unsaved person as someone at enmity with God, which makes it clear that no relationship can exist between an unsaved person and God.

Adam represented all of humanity when he sinned. All people thereafter are born separated from God. Humanity as a whole, has an identity crisis. It is a systemic crisis whereby mankind is unable, in our own strength and wisdom, to recreate our once perfect identity in God. Scripture describes mankind without God as an "orphan". People who are separated from God because of sin, are broken and without direction, double-minded, lost, suspicious of everyone else, and susceptible to the devil's temptations. These temptations are disguised attempts by the devil to draw mankind into all kinds of pseudo destructive relationships, which eventually either completely distort the person's identity or destroy the person entirely.

Because of people's ignorance of God, they refuse to turn to God our Creator and find what we need. Instead, we try to find the loving acceptance only God can give in others around us, who are in the same predicament and are also searching for the same life-giving affirmation. This inner hunger, which is driving mankind's need to do something to feel valued, is a powerful urge. In my view it is stronger than mankind's natural 'fight or flight' instinct, designed to ensure survival. The core desire for acceptance goes beyond man's desire to live.

Many of the human achievements in the Guinness World Records book are proof of man's desire to be noticed by others. Many of the achievements listed are proof of people's desire to feel good about themselves. The highly sought-after internal sense of accomplishment, created by ever-increasing dangerous activities, is a stimulant more powerful than morphine to an injured person. Unfortunately, once the approval-seeking person has tasted the wow of the crowds, their appetite for applause grows by the day. But those desiring acceptance will never have their thirst quenched until they hear the Creator, the all-loving Father of all, speak words of affirmation over them as they answer His call to be reconciled to Him through His Son Jesus.

Every person, apart from Adam, who has entered and will enter this world, enters it with a specific predisposition regarding relationships. A predisposition is something that causes a person to suffer from an existing condition. What this means is that because of their sin in the Garden of Eden, mankind has a broken understanding of what a true relationship with God and with others should be. Unfortunately, people base their theories, views and arguments on this predisposition.

It is necessary to first understand the value of a true relationship, and we can do this by looking at the process a newborn baby goes through. When the baby is developing in the mother's womb, it relies on what the mother ate and drank for its sustenance. Subsequent to the baby's birth, it is still totally reliant on the mother for sustenance, and over time the baby grows into a child and eventually an adult. Although the baby matures, it never loses its relationship with its mother. All that changes are the needs of the baby, now an adult. In a similar way, mankind is totally dependent on God. What man's sinful predisposition refers to is that sin reprogrammed man's thinking that either we can exist without God, or, as many Christians do, they have a spiritual encounter with God and thereafter live similar to that of a deist. Mankind was created by God to relate to God. The way to relate does not come packaged with birth. It has to be taught to every person using what God has given us to do so – the Bible.

Natural parents can speak acceptance over their child, but what is truly needed is for a child at a mature age to hear that God values and accepts them. Without this, people pursue all kinds of ways to make a name for themselves to achieve some sort of acceptance from others, when in fact, every individual yearns for the acceptance of their Father in heaven.

Being accepted fulfils a yearning most people do not know exists in their inmost being. The need for acceptance cannot enable the person to fulfil it, otherwise we would have done so long ago. The need for this affirmation is what drives people to searching for it in various ways. Doing things to be seen and performing to an audience to receive an applause make people feel unique. I recently heard a man who had most of his body covered with tattoos say, "It makes me feel unique. People always ask me about the signs on my body." What this desperate man was crying out for was acceptance and being valued by others.

People's urge for what God has placed deep inside of them is something only God can fulfil. This is what the devil attacked in Genesis 3:5 when he said they did not need God. He suggested that they become gods unto themselves and that they had no need of a 'Father' at all. Satan's deceptive argument was that mankind can be a god. He succeeded in doing this by painting a false portrait of what it would be like in the future if mankind was their own ruler. Because of man's fascination with the forbidden fruit, they ate and fell into disobedience and rebellion against God. Their relationship with God was in shreds and they were banished from the Garden of Eden.

God had a plan to restore mankind back to Himself – a complete plan of reconciliation whereby He would pay the price for man's sin. God's plan is based in His love for every individual. This plan restores mankind back to their Maker, their eternal Father. Christ died for every person on earth. God makes a strong statement about the individual when He says that the number of hairs on our heads are counted by Him. If the individual was not important to God, Jesus would not have paid attention to the repentant sinner on the cross next to him. To God every individual is unique. This is true, not because of who the individual is, but because of who God is.

Chapter 15

Not by works

B elievers who have found their true identity in God and who are rooted in Christ, display an interesting characteristic; because they know that God loves and accepts them, they do not strive to prove themselves to God or their fellow man anymore. Their works focus on what God has called them to. They humbly seek no approval from their fellow man. They do not copy nor covet another person's ministry, gifts, talents, methods or revelation (1 Peter 4:10). The good works (Ephesians 2:10) they perform are a result of their salvation; not a way to gain salvation.

When looking at how Paul views the believer's works, he did not say believers are to count their works. He warned that their works should be of such a nature that it would withstand God's fire-test on judgement day (1 Corinthians 3:10-15). Our relationship with God is based on the love He shows us. We reciprocate this love by the good works we perform, which are tangible proof of this relationship we have with God. The good works, or the lack thereof, will not influence our identity in Christ. Any child born into a family cannot become more or less of a son or daughter by their good deeds or perhaps misdeeds. They will always remain a child of the house.

God the Father, through His Son Jesus, accepts all who approach Him unconditionally. However, because every individual is born in sin, mankind has great difficulty accepting God. Born without a relationship with God, it is natural for people with such a disposition to develop distrust in God. Through this distrust we find ourselves living apart from and distant from God. This inherent disposition has trained mankind to be self-serving, independent, and arrogant enough to declare their own self-righteousness. It takes time in the life of any new believer to truly accept God. This might sound strange, but even when people are born again, they unknowingly continually strive for God's approval by performing noble acts of service and worship. Salvation is by grace through faith, not by works so that no man could boast. That is the only way mankind can obtain a relationship with God. Salvation cannot be obtained by performing noble tasks; nor can it be secured through merely expressing the desire thereof. Some of the benefits of this relationship is sonship, acceptance, approval, identity and eternal rest.

Mankind cannot function without God. Our relationship with God is the highest calling of man. It is here where we experience eternal peace, purpose and rest. Here our identity is complete in the way God intended from the day He created us. The opposite is also true: An independent person without a relationship with God is like a fish out of water – our very existence is tormented by anxiety. We have no hope because life is not in our hands.

Since Genesis 3:22, when God had no choice but to banish mankind from His presence, humanity has been left with a desperate desire to be reunited to his Maker and Friend. Our deepest desire is relationship, which is a God-given expression of love. Because relational connectedness is a key aspect in man's existence, we have within us a burning desire to restore what has been lost, we try to befriend objects to fill the hunger for companionship. No earthly object or relationship can replace what God Himself built into man. Even the most cold-blooded killer loves his own family. Even a man like Adolf Hitler, who passionately hated all Jews, had the capacity to passionately love Eva Anna Paula Braun (Hitler). Even the loudest advocates of atheism love their children. Relational love is a key attribute of God Himself, which He built into all of mankind. No matter how mankind tries to deny the existence of God, our connection to God, and our dependency on Him will always reflect love, life and compassion in some way during our daily life.

People incorrectly label God with the devil's wrongdoing. By believing this lie, mankind has walked away from God and embarked on a journey of fear, deceit and denial. Through the devil's lies, the enemy has created a perception that either God does not exist or that God is to blame for the brokenness of mankind and creation. This might cause people to run away from God, but our desperation for relational love drives us to other avenues to find acceptance, love and fulfilment. We enslave and burden ourselves with thing like sport, money, positions of power, music, sex, and careers. The burning desire within us to relate is extremely powerful, and we can observe people's level of desperation in how they spend their time – the avenues they create to give and receive love, affirmation, identity, being valued, appreciated and accepted.

The principle of 'doing'

Many religions are centred around the principle of 'doing', promoting an inner purity when their followers perform certain activities. The way to salvation is not through doing, but through surrendering all we do and all we are. The way of obtaining a right-standing before God is by believing in what Jesus accomplished on our behalf. Without this belief, we become anxious to be cleansed from our inherent fallen state, and we perform actions to achieve inner peace. These actions can make the doer feel good, and it is plausible that this feeling of accomplishment can take place in the absence of a deity's approval. The more these self-assigned activities are performed, the more the flesh boasts, which then leads to self-entitlement, self-justification, and a claim of self-righteousness. Where we see the elevation of 'self', we are reminded of Paul's grave warnings against boasting in the flesh (1 Corinthians 1:29; 2 Corinthians 11:18; Galatians 6:14; Ephesians 2:9; Philippians 3:1-4).

Whether a person performs activities religiously or in the workplace, the same principle applies: God made mankind and gave him works to perform. The relationship preceded the works handed out. Mankind became confused and separated religious from secular work, in the sense that since we fell in sin, we have attempted to purify ourselves through works in the absence of a relationship. Neither religious nor secular works can accomplish Christian salvation. In the context of other religions, the principle of 'salvation' might mean an inner purity, achieving mind over body control, obtaining higher knowledge, and so forth.

We can ask if, in the context of relationships, God is pleased with the person who performs the works, whether religious or in the workplace? And, at what point does the person ever gain an assurance that they have done enough to warrant God's favour and approval? The opposite is also true. If God is a relational God, does it not make sense that no matter how much you work, you can never 'purchase' His approval based on your labours. This means that true contentment is not based on works but on the approval of a loving Father.

The peace of God

If a person's approval is found within their relationship with God, then true joy and contentment will fill the worker's daily life, no matter what they do. If the relationship precedes the work or religious activities, then, as Jesus said in John 20:19, 21, 22, a peace will develop within the person (see also Ephesians 2:10 which shows that good works are the fruit of a relationship with God). This is a peace that governs a person's life. It is a peace no one else but the Spirit of God can give. This peace reflects a reconciliation with God on a relational level, which ushers in His peace when we perform any work. Once the relationship between a person and God has been restored, all that person does from then on, is not done to achieve God's favour and blessings, but is an outflow of his joy and thanksgiving to God.

True contentment, peace and joy in our workplaces and religious activities are an outflow of a healthy relationship with our Father, not *vice versa*. Man's desperation to be restored to God the eternal Father can be compared to a sailor abandoned at sea, surrounded by water, yet without a drop to drink. Eventually, in desperation, he drinks the salty water knowing it is bad for his health. The lonely sailor will suffer a slow and excruciating death.

In this vein, many people will consume the poison around them – the empty promises, the distant mirages of happiness, the quick-fix solutions, and the false hopes offered by advertising campaigns. Like the sea water surrounding the stranded sailor, this is tempting, but hopeless. Paul warns us in 1 Timothy 6:9-10 that people who pursue the distractions this world offers, unwisely punish themselves with many griefs. This world is doomed to eternal destruction and so is everything it offers. In the words of Jesus to the Samaritan woman at the well, "Whoever drinks the water I gave them will never thirst" (John 4:14ᵃ NIV). Mankind's deepest desperate urge is not to perform more and more works in order to achieve an elevated state of being, it is to be united with our Creator.

The rest God gives

In 1 Peter 3:18, Peter says that Christ, the righteous One, was the once-off sacrifice to remove sin. He did this so that we, the unrighteous, can be reconciled to God. This reconciliation is the relationship every believer yearns for and from it all works transpire. The fellowship offered to us by God, through His Son, is what provides a peace, a trust, and a rest no one else but the Father can give. The rest Jesus speaks of in Matthew 11:28 is when our relationship with God is established and growing, and it is the opposite to people's fruitless efforts to save themselves. God executed His plan to live within us. In doing so He has declared us His people.

The summary of man's desperate urge is our pursuit of the illusive rest. All our works drive us to more uncertainty regarding our standing with our eternal Father, which can lead to great frustration and anger. It is hope deferred that makes a person inwardly sick. The more people strive to attain acceptance through their own actions, the further they drift from the Father.

God demonstrated His ways to us in Genesis 2:2. After He created, He rested. This is a rest only God can give mankind. It is a rest that originates with God, not mankind. Any attempt to keep working in order to achieve peace, will wear a person out.

A son in his father's house does not need to prove that he is a son. Both the father and the son would be frustrated if this was needed. No, a son behaves like a son in his father's house by being who he has been made to be and he understand his acceptance and belonging in the family. There is nothing he needs to prove. When the son begins to live in what God created him to be, then he can do what God has called him to. Works performed by a believer who is secure in their identity in Christ are similar to a son in his father's house – he is at rest and does not attempt to prove his sonship.

Only a person's identity in Christ can bring godly peace and rest to the person. They do not strive to prove anything to anyone. Being secure in Christ brings a rest that money cannot buy. It settles a great internal battle within mankind; a deep longing and desperate search for the One true God – the Father of all. Once this urge has been settled, the person's relationship with their Father in heaven helps them hear their Father's will. From this moment on, the deeds performed by the believer, please the Father's heart and give great rest to the believer.

Chapter 16

The pain of rejection

The cover of this book shows a bridegroom who is about to say his vows to his bride. During the declaration of the bridegroom's vows to his bride, he expresses three things to her. He declares, in the presence of witnesses, that he accepts her, appreciates her and values her as she is. These aspects are what every person on earth desires and needs. They make us secure and boost our self-worth.

As much as these three aspects build someone up, the opposite is rejection, which is a force deep within every person that is so destructive it can destroy the person and those around them. The destructive power of rejection has been seen in countless lives, and especially in the lives of leaders who have fallen prey to the internal workings of rejection.

Rejection is an unseen sense that every person has as a result of Adam's sin and what it caused. Adam and Eve were banished from God's presence because of sin. Since then, rejection can cause severe trauma to people's self-worth. Not only does the victim of rejection suffer, but they also cause others to suffer greatly. The effects of rejection in a person's life are in many cases traceable in their children and their children's children.

Noel and Phyl Gibson, authors of *Excuse me... Your Rejection is Showing*, said: "The greatest undiagnosed and therefore untreated malady today is rejection."

Rejection establishes a foothold for the enemy to cause pain in the person's heart. They begin to believe the lie and try to compensate for it. Have we perhaps underestimated the effect rejection has on people's ability to relate to God and others? Perhaps humanity has been looking in the wrong place in their searching for the reason for mankind's relational problems.

In Jesus' final hour on the cross, He cried: "My God, my God, why have you forsaken me?"(Matthew 27:46). With this, Jesus, the Son of God, again felt the bitter taste of rejection. He was introduced to rejection from an early age. While He was in Mary's womb, the child Jesus was suspected of being conceived out of wedlock. At two years old, King Herod sought his life. Rejected by his family, the religious leaders and most of the Jewish community, Jesus knew what it felt like to be rejected. Even the Son of God felt the pain of being rejected, yet He did not fall into the devil's trap to retaliate. He humbled Himself even unto death (Philippians 2:8).

Rejection is a silent force that creeps deep into the heart of a person. It is able to rewire a person's psychological behaviour where a peaceful individual can become a person who sets out to hurt themselves and others. They do this in an attempt to cope with the tremendous pain they carry. In many cases, a person who has felt rejected reaches a stage where the lies the devil tells them make them believe the whole world is against them. The enemy is a master at using the opportunity when we experience rejection to plant lies in our hearts and then incite us to respond in ways that are damaging, thereby increasing the problem.

Rejection can cause a person to react in several ways. Either they deny what they are suffering, or they project it onto others, or they find coping mechanisms to help them deal with the pain. Some of the coping mechanisms are violence, control, aggression, retribution, anger and bitterness. If left untreated, these mechanisms can lead to damaging results in the person and those around them.

The process of dealing with rejection begins in the heart with reconciliation. Rejection causes a scar in a person's life, which affects virtually all the relationships they enter into. For instance, if a father speaks negative words over his children, the scars of those words affect their own marriages and the lives of their own children. The effects of rejection are not initially visible in the relationship, but in time, with enough pressure and triggers, the wounds of rejection begin to resurface as the person tries to defend themselves against criticism. Any fingers pointed at them are seen as attacks and are taken very seriously.

Rejection can cut deep into a person's heart, especially when it comes from someone in authority, such as church leaderships, teachers or spouses. One of the fruits of rejection is hatred, or intense of others. The dislike can be triggered by an unhappiness a person carries regarding their physical appearance, or perhaps hurts suffered by the hand or mouth of a parent. People either internalise these feelings of hurt and become introverted, or they slowly implode. Others externalise the hurt and in turn hurt others. The very thing they despise in others, they become themselves. They project their rejection towards others in an attempt to make themselves more acceptable.

Many marriages, which start with a beautiful ceremony and the exchange of intimate vows, last for only a short while and then abruptly end. The scars of rejection suffered while growing up, psychological injuries incurred from a previous marriage, surface and the once-romantic couple see their dream fade away as one of the spouses withdraws. No words are necessarily uttered. Rejection has made intimacy impossible. In many cases, gender-based violence is a direct result of rejection. A marriage and the resultant family see the greatest measures of rejection and the retaliatory pain that go with rejection. The main reason for this is that rejection is found exclusively in a relational setting. Rejection and the poison it spreads was never created by God. In the Trinity where perfect unity has forever existed, sin was never present, and therefore rejection did not emanate from God. Rejection is a direct result of sin, which originates from Satan (Ezekiel 28:15).

What was Jesus' focus?

Matthew 1:21 tells us exactly why Jesus came – what His mission was. It was to remove sin from God's people. We can easily stop here when we do not read Scripture in a holistic way. The removal of sin had a deeper meaning. God's love, as expressed in John 3:16, was the removal of sin, which was the barrier to an eternal relationship with every believer. Where we go wrong is that we want to understand love and relationships from our earthly point of view. The loving relationship God has in mind is far above our earthly understanding. In order to restore mankind's relationship with God, He came up with the greatest 'peace' plan ever – the sacrifice of His Son to do away with the hostilities between God and mankind.

Love does not exist apart from a relationship. 1 John 4:8 tells us that God is love. It does not say God has love. From this we understand that God is relational. Everything God creates stems from this principle, which means that we are also relational beings.

In Galatians 5:22-23 we read what the fruit of the Spirit is – the attributes we demonstrate when we have the Spirit of fellowship (2 Corinthians 12:13). We cannot manufacture the fruit of the Spirit; they are what we begin to demonstrate when we have the Spirit of God within us. The fruit we bear is the evidence of the Spirit's work in the life of a believer. The Spirit of God is also called the Spirit of fellowship, therefore, the more fruit a person bears, the closer the relationship that person has with the Spirit of God.

How we relate to a God we cannot see

How do we as believers build a relationship with a God we cannot see, hug or touch? How do we know what He wants from us and how can we maintain a healthy relationship with Him? Where do we learn what angers Him and what He despises? How do we know what He loves best and enjoys? No other source of information can compare to God's inerrant Word. All we need for a godly life is in Scripture.

Peter says in his second epistle that God's divine power has given us all we need for a godly life through our knowledge of Christ (2 Peter 1:3). How do we gain knowledge regarding Jesus? We study the Bible from Genesis to Revelation. This knowledge, as Jesus said, will be like seeds of life germinating in our hearts and we will begin to grow in our understanding of God.

The Old Testament is crucial. It tells us what grows and destroys our relationship with God. Early on in Genesis 3 we see that sin separates us from God. It caused Adam and Eve to die and until today, it causes death to mankind. God had to deal with sin and because of their fall, mankind lost their standing and relationship with God and embarked on a self-righteous, self-seeking and self-steering path that destroys lives.

For us to understand how to relate to a God we cannot see or touch, we need to look at how God dealt with Israel as a nation. What we see is similar to how a mother treats her newborn. At birth she satisfies the infant's need for food and protection. It is the closeness to the mother that cements their relationship. As a group of slaves, Israel cried out to God for 400 years before He delivered them. God saved them from Egyptian slavery and became their 'nursing mother'. From the outset of their journey, God saw to their basic needs of food, water and protection. He fought against Pharaoh who pursued them after they departed from his slave camps, He fed them manna and quails, and He taught them that one of His names was God their Provider. God wanted them to rely on Him, to wait for Him, to expect good things from and trust Him fully. These aspects are what builds a relationship between a mother and her infant – and a new believer and God. Time and again, God fought on their behalf and destroyed their enemies. We see in Numbers 20:12 how much God values His people trusting Him.

We see that a crucial aspect of any relationship is trust. Hebrews 3:19 makes a startling statement. It says that most of the Israelites who left Egypt did not enter the Promised Land because they did not trust God's ability to bring them to it. They did not rely on Him or His promises. This reliance and trust can be described as faith. Faith is the principle throughout Scripture that healed people, described God's people, set people aside from others, and explained who the people were whose God would fight for them and provide for them. In Hebrews 11:6, it explains who is in a relationship with God.

How do we show our faith in a God we cannot see or touch? When we extrapolate the principle of the Ten Commandments God gave to Israel in the New Testament, we see that Jesus is said to be an exact representation of the Father (Hebrews 1:3). What we do with Jesus today is what the Israelites did with God's laws back in the Old Testament. Ignoring and disobeying them caused them eternal harm. Ignoring and disobeying Jesus will cause every person the same harm today. God expected Israel to follow His laws, and teach them to their children and their children's children. This is how Israel showed their love for God – by obeying His laws. Jesus makes exactly the same statement in John 14:15 and equates loving Him to obeying His commandments.

Obey and follow them and it will go well with you (Deuteronomy 12:28). It gave the nation of Israel 'handles' on how to love, goals to work towards, and things to do and watch out for. The Laws God gave also created helpful boundaries they were not to transgress. When we read God's commandments, we see that the Israelites had to depend on God for everything. He led, fed, and protected them. When God related to Israel, He described them as His bride, His people, His children, and so on. His description of Israel made it clear that He did not see them as a distant group of people; His intention was for them to be as close as His family. If anyone hurt them, they might as well have hurt God Himself.

The word I want to highlight is 'dependent'. In Jesus' parable of the lost son in Luke 15, we read of a father and his two sons, demonstrating a loving relationship between father and son. We tend to focus on the son and his actions in the story, and don't often stop and ponder how the father must have felt when his son asked for his share of his father's estate. It means he had lost the relationship he once had with his father and now sees his father as dead – while he was still alive – and the son rejected his father's care and wisdom. Towards the end of the parable, we see how the son is restored to his father's house and care.

God calls us His friends. He never intended for believers to be mere servants, people who perform tasks out of respect or fear, but to be in close relationship with Himself. In many ways it resembles the men of Athens in Acts 17 who had many gods, yet those gods were distant to mankind. When we read how God dwelt among the people of Israel during the forty-year wilderness walk, we see the opposite of a distant and removed deity. He pursues His people in their good and bad times. Genesis 3 shows us that immediately after Adam sinned, God pursued him despite Adam's rebellion and disobedience.

Kept for later

In 1 Corinthians 2:9-10, Paul mentions that God has prepared (Isaiah 64:4) something amazing for those who love Him, something that no eye has seen, no ear has heard, nor could the mind of any person conceive of it. Paul says the door to this amazing reward is love. And for this reason, he says in verse 10 that God has revealed it to us by His Spirit of fellowship. Paul is saying that only within a relationship with God will we be able to partake in God's plan for every believer. He adds that within the Trinity's relational existence, the Spirit searches God's wisdom and reveals it to those who love Him. It is therefore clear that the secrets God has prepared will only be revealed to those He knows and trusts.

Trust as a sign

Why is Job in the Bible? Why would a man suffer so much and still be God's friend? What do we learn about friendship with God from Job? We see that Job was tested when God allowed him to be tempted and his testing focused on the strength of his trust in God. Both his wife and his friends urged him to forsake God, but Job saw beyond the losses of his children, material possessions, and status and kept his trust in God. Any relationship is built on trust and the way to evaluate trust is to have it tested. This way it not only deepens, as was the case with Job, but it demonstrated to God that Job was worthy of deeper understanding regarding his relationship with God.

Helpful scaffolding

In constructing a building, contractors use scaffolding, which are temporary tools and are not part of the building. Visible on the outside, they assist builders for a season. Scaffolding is similar to the cocoon a worm constructs around itself in order to pass into the butterfly phase. Once the transformation or construction is complete, the cocoon or scaffolding is not needed anymore. What is left is the final product for all to see. The timeframe of a building process is similar to that of a relationship, which undergoes several developmental phases – no completed building is left with the temporary scaffolding around it.

Looking at the process of salvation, we need to understand that being born again is not the fullness of God's plan for us. God's plan is to complete the work He has started in the life of every believer. The plan of salvation God has affected through His Son Jesus, is a plan of reconciliation between God and man (2 Corinthians 5:18). God's focus is the restoration of a relationship with mankind, and He has gone to great lengths to accomplish this. God is love and as we have said in this book, love does not exist in a void. Love exists within the framework of a relationship; God is love and if love functions within a relationship, then God is all for it.

Love, within the framework of the relationship between God and man, had to be rebuilt. After the relational breakdown, God took many years to reveal Himself as the God of love. In John 3:16 Jesus was explaining to Nicodemus that God so loved the world that He was pouring out His Son as an atoning sacrifice to restore mankind back to Himself. Jesus came to pay the price to remove sin from the life of everyone who would believe in Him. By this action, God has restored true love in the heart of every believer. God is love and therefore cannot stop loving us. We are the ones who fell into sin and who stopped loving and obeying God. Once sin, which is the reason mankind was banished from God's presence, has been removed, the relationship with God can be restored.

In 1 Corinthians 13, described as the chapter of love, Paul mentions the tools we need to develop love. In verse 13 he says God has given us hope, faith and love, and that of these, love is the greatest. Hope and faith are there to build what is most precious to God, which is relational love. In verse 8 he says, "Love never ends."

All the other tools used to construct a solid relationship will become redundant in the same way scaffolding around a building become redundant after the building has been completed. In verses 11 to 12 Paul explains that while our relationship with God is not fully matured, we need the scaffolding to help us develop our relationship with God. While we are on this earth and know in part, the scaffolding God has given us serves a valuable purpose. Yet a day will come when we either pass on or when Jesus returns to fetch His bride, then we will be complete as Paul says in verse 12. Once we behold God, we will have a fullness in our relationship with Him and we will no longer require the scaffolding used to construct our relationship with God. The tools of faith and hope will become redundant, and we will know God as He has known us from the beginning (verse 12).

It is therefore worth it all to pursue our relationship with God to the fullest, and use hope and faith as scaffolding to construct what would one day become eternal.

Chapter 17

Love and the Law

How do we initiate and grow a relationship? Who takes the first step? In the context of a parent and child – it's the parent who first supplies an infant's basic needs and then later begins to instruct them on rules and regulations. Imagine a child is fed from infancy, yet never instructed regarding social rules and practices. Many parents run the risk of failing to instil rules on how to behave in and outside their homes in the lives of their children. Rules like respecting their parents, honouring older people, honesty, guarding what they see, respecting others, self-control, and many more. These rules will ensure that their relationships with their parents and others remain healthy.

In the same way, God rescued a nation from slavery. He took them in as His own and began the long process of training them to abide in a relationship with Him. How did God train them? He first rescued them from slavery and then gave them the Ten Commandments and other laws they were to observe. These laws and commandments were not meant to take God's place, but to create a specific attitude in them to honour God in everything they do, possess, and speak. These laws reflected the holiness of God, and were to be upheld in order to maintain their relationship with God. They were tools to promote freedom and a way to ensure the presence of God remained with them, which in turn, ensured peace and prosperity.

Unfortunately, people began seeing these laws and commandments as the relationship itself and in doing so, created a burden for themselves of striving for perfection through their own efforts. The Law was meant to govern the relationship by giving people practical 'handles' on what to do to maintain it. Fulfilling the Law made people feel empowered and proud. It boosted egos; it made them feel self-fulfilled and they became self-centred. The danger here was that the Law began taking the place of the second person in the relationship. Although God was the author of the Law and the giver of life, people exchanged the fellowship of God for the approval of God.

If we base our relationship on how well we uphold God's commandments, we have created a system of self-justification in which we pride ourselves in our achievements. When we score our own performance, we run the risk of creating a false expectation of God's approval. We even begin to build a false identity on how much we estimate God appreciates our upholding the Law. We embark on a journey of striving for perfection instead of growing in a loving relationship with God. The Law both opposes and removes God's unconditional love. This is because, when we manage to maintain the Law in our own efforts, we become proud. When we fail to observe the Law, we become angry with God for expecting perfection from us.

Love is higher than the Law.

The Law given to Israel in Exodus 20:3-17 is preceded by the declaration of God's unconditional love. Love is a gift we receive from God our Father – it is a free gift from God that we neither deserve nor work for. Love is therefore not achieved through the observation of a Law. In a home, love is bestowed by a parent on a child before the child has a reciprocal ability. Similarly, God bestowed love on us while we were still His enemies. He demonstrated this by sending His Son to die for sinners and thereafter He sent the Holy Spirit to establish love within our hearts at the moment of our new birth.

When we look at God's dealings with Israel, we see how He liberated them from slavery and provided for all their needs as they journeyed into the Wilderness. Their relationship was not initiated when He covenanted with them at Mount Sinai. His relationship with Israel started much earlier. This means, the commandments He gave the nation of Israel at Mount Sinai were not to assist in building a relationship. Rather, they were to maintain the relationship already established. No matter what a child does, true parents cannot help but to love their child. Not success nor defeat can add or take away a parent's love for a child.

What this means to us is that we should not view the Laws of God as a means to build a relationship with Him. The laws are there to maintain our relationship with God. If we are to keep score on how we are doing, we would score the way the Pharisees did. All they received as a reward was a rebuke from Jesus. He said that they, as with all the other believers, are to approach Him as a person relationally, not through their careful observation of the Law and the Scriptures (John 5:39). Jesus wanted to build a relationship with the disciples, which was totally different from the rulers of the age who lorded it over their subjects. To be relationally connected to God does not depend on the observation of a set of laws; it is a gift of God called grace and it is free. Thereafter it is the relationship of the believer to deepen the relationship by studying the Laws of God to better understand what improves or harms the relationship.

Our relationship with God is governed by His laws, not our performance, and it is based on God as a person, not on the object of the laws. An object can never take the place of a person. When we establish our relationship on God's love for us, we empower ourselves to fulfil the Law out of our reciprocal loving appreciation for what God has and is doing for us. Through this we live a life of peace because we do not find our identity or value in what we do. The opposite is also true. We cannot be deprived of our heavenly Father's presence because of our failures.

Testing in a relationship

Life for any believer will be full of opportunities to grow, and these opportunities come in the form of daily tests. They are seldom pleasant, especially while we are in the midst of them. However, when we look back, we agree they were necessary to develop us. Any believer who lives with the expectation that life is one smooth ride will soon be proved wrong. Testing is an absolute necessity in the life of the believer. Scripture makes it clear that God allows us to be tested. See Deuteronomy 8:2; Psalms 26:2; Jeremiah 17:10 and James 1:3 for some examples.

It is also clear in God's Word that He does not tempt us. Testing is meant to develop us, while temptation is meant to destroy us. It is not difficult to see that God being a loving Father always has our development and not our destruction in mind. It is during testing that a person either fails or develops the ability to master their weak fleshly nature. Testing is a furnace that purifies our faith in God.

When we look at other relationships like marriage and platonic friendships, we see that the strength of a relationship can only be measured after it has withstood testing. As with any load-bearing substance, its strength can only be determined when it is placed under pressure.

We see how God tested Adam and Eve by allowing them to be tempted by the serpent. God tested Job's faith by allowing the devil to attack him in many areas of his life. Abraham was tested when God asked him to leave his father's house to journey to a foreign land. He was also tested when God asked him to sacrifice his son Isaac. God tested the Israelites in the Wilderness on their way to the Promised Land. Hebrews 3:19 tells us that when tested, many of the Israelites' faith failed and they were refused entry into the Promised Land. Jesus tested His disciples' faith by asking them to feed a multitude; to have faith in Him during the storm; to remain awake in prayer in the Garden of Gethsemane; to believe in His promised resurrection; and in many other instances.

When we consider the importance of our God-given relationships, we cannot remove the need for any relationship to be tested. We must understand that God is not surprised when we grow or fail during a test; He allows tests to take place in our lives and then uses their outcome to speak to us. Sometimes this is the only way we are able to hear God speak to us. It's difficult to convince a person to abandon an ill-fated idea, especially when they are convinced they are right. In many instances, it is only after they have experienced defeat that they are open to outside influence.

Testing is part and parcel of any relationship. It is meant to cement the relationship through the process of exposing weaknesses and advocating for change in those areas. Testing brings the parties in a relationship closer together because it builds trust as the individuals in the relationship abandon other possibilities to show deep trust and faithfulness towards one another.

It cuts to the heart

'It cuts to the heart' might seem a controversial statement, but the aim is to show that relationships have the potential to cause more suffering in a person than any physical suffering. Relationships are what we all desire, but we sometimes forget that these relational commitments do not come with warning stickers.

It is not only humans who have relational struggles. We see in Scripture that Satan rebelled against God, bringing Satan in direct conflict with God – the fallout caused a third of the angels in heaven to be expelled from God's presence. This rebellion was a demand for self-rule. Satan desired God's throne and was expelled for doing so. His act did not stop there. He deceived Adam and Eve into believing the same lie – the desire for self-determination. It is a belief that creation does not need the Creator; a foolish belief rooted in Satan's original crime. The root of this crime is a break in trust – a violation of intimate trust. It not only brings pain and regret to mankind, it brings pain and regret to God's heart too. We see God expressing pain and regret after observing man's wickedness in the earth (Genesis 6:6). This pain and grief relates to the nature of sin, which separates mankind from God. The separation began with Adam and Eve and subsequently appeared in the lives of their descendants.

God called the nation of Israel His bride – one of the most intimate expressions of a relational union in Scripture – and we can read about God's frustration when they rebelled. And yet, Scripture also tells us of God's abundant grace for His people. The moment Adam fell into sin, God did not destroy everything and start over. God as Creator-Father was patient and introduced a plan of salvation.

When God speaks about Israel as He does, we see the extent of His love for His people.

God Himself, in Deuteronomy 1:32-36 and Psalms 78, describes His relationship with Israel and how they have caused Him hurt – this despite all He had done for them. The point I am making is that nothing can cut as deep into our hearts as a relationship in which the parties do not honour and consider one another.

Pseudo relationships

Since mankind's fall into sin, they have been banished from God's presence. This banishment meant mankind lost their relationship with God on a daily basis. As explained earlier regarding God's journey with Israel from Egyptian Slavery, through the Wilderness and into the Promised Land, God was teaching Israel how to establish, maintain and grow relationships with Himself and with others around them.

What we see early in the history of Israel is the creation of idols and the people of God devoting themselves to worshipping these manmade images. We sometimes look on these activities and wonder why they allowed this to happen to themselves. It was never a sudden move. It had to do with their upbringing; the influences around them and ignorance. These things slowly and systematically drew Israel away from God and eventually caused a complete breakdown in relations.

Today, we, as the people of God, share the same history as others who do not believe in God. We all begin life as humans who attempt to live apart from God, self-reliant and self-sufficient in our own limited knowledge. We use our imaginations to replace God's presence. In the modern world we live in, we busy ourselves with all kinds of activities such as Facebook, Twitter, other social networks, music, sport, entertainment, jobs, and many more. These activities rob us of the time we were meant to spend with God. We get addicted to our social network fix every morning as we wake up. Our message check-in now happens before our first caffeine fix. The human race is now busier than ever. The amount of data we consume and information we receive is at its highest ever. We spend more time on the small god Google, researching and searching for answers to temporary problems than we spend with the real God, searching for eternal answers to our problems. Consumerism has been taken to a higher level by the internet giving us access to millions of products, which at the click of a button, we buy and have delivered to our doorstep.

We have fallen victim to one of the most corrosive elements that dissolves any relationship, which is busyness and distractions. For many young couples, a TV in the bedroom initially does not pose a threat. Yet later on in their marriage they are still two strangers who have not learnt how to communicate and become each other's best friends. The distraction in their relationship provides hundreds of channels they can browse and vegetate for hours. Although they are next to each other physically, they have grown apart from each other emotionally. If we take this example of a TV in a couple's bedroom, we can learn from it and begin to understand what distractions can cause in our much-needed relationship with God. People's interests, hobbies, families, careers, talents and many other distractions prevent them from building a relationship with God.

It is alarming that we as Christians misunderstand some of the principles God has given us. These principles, although they originate in heaven, are critically important for us as believers. They are principles such as propitiation, imputation and expiation, which are steps in the process of reconciliation between God and man. As critical as they are, they are not the focus of what we need to be taught. When we as believers overemphasise these steps, we begin to lose sight of the real goal God intended for us. This goal is found in the word 'reconciliation'. This word hints at something that is broken and needs fixing.

Reconciliation is the process of reconnecting two estranged parties, using steps such as propitiation, imputation and expiation. Once we have been taught these principles, which are foundational to walking with God, we need to put them into practice to grow our relationship with God. When we elevate the individual steps over the entire process we are in error. It could be compared to a newly married couple who overemphasise their wedding ceremony by revisiting the venue, the photographs in their albums and the vows they took. They focus on only one step that was meant to lead them to a growing relationship. And years later they remain strangers, unable to communicate their desires, frustrations, and hopes, and they are equally incapable of communicating in times of conflict.

All of this shows us how true relationships need to be initiated, developed and maintained towards maturity. Distractions and outside influences can be harmful to the development of any relationship, which will show up on the day of reckoning. In the context of a marriage, a day will come when all we have built will be tested. During marriage counselling sessions, a crucial remedy has always proven to be the quality of communication the couple has to develop over time. Those who have invested in their relationships are able to address misunderstandings and conflict much easier than those who have not.

Similarly, a day will come when the bridge we have built between God and ourselves will be tested. If we have allowed ourselves to be distracted by many irrelevant activities, we will suffer the greatest loss.

Part Five

What Jesus did

Chapter 18

Your place of authority

J esus was followed by large crowds. He also had friends – people He loved and cared about a great deal, like Lazarus, Mary and Martha, who on many occasions opened their house to Him. Jesus also had many disciples. Some He specifically chose, while others followed Him because of their faith in His Messianic teachings. He had a large group of followers, perhaps 120 or so. Yet He intentionally spent most of His time with the twelve. He regularly drew them away from the crowds and to Himself. Jesus deposited His life and work into the lives of His disciples. During these times, He sowed His divine seed of the Word of God into their hearts. Later on, the 120 waiting in the Upper Room, were empowered by His Spirit. My point is that it was with His twelve closest disciples, whom Jesus designated apostles, that He would later entrust His entire ministry to. He shared the hidden aspects of the Kingdom of God with them and not with the crowds. The twelve apostles would begin to expand the Kingdom of God to the entire world.

Of the twelve, He made a special effort with three specific disciples, namely Peter, James and John. During this time Jesus ploughed into the lives of these unschooled and rough men. He questioned what needed to be questioned, He pointed out fears and weaknesses, and He saw in them the potential to change the world. At some point Jesus even told them they could leave if they wanted to. Some did, but in John 6:68-69 (NIV) Peter makes the following statement: "Lord, to whom shall we go? You have the words of eternal life. We have come to believe and to know you are the Holy One of God." Peter, in a way, stood his ground, where Adam in Genesis 3 failed during temptation. Peter did not say "Where shall we go?" referring to another place of instruction or teaching. By that time, Peter had begun to realise that Jesus was no ordinary man. He also understood that the relationship that he and the others had with Jesus was life-giving. This bond they had with Jesus was the door to true joy and it built a bridge to where the transforming teachings of Jesus could reach them. It was for this reason that Peter would not leave Jesus.

Despite the direct and sometimes painful personal adjustments Jesus made in Peter's character and life, Peter loved Jesus and refused to leave. The difficulty in turning the life of a person, like Peter the fisherman, one hundred and eighty degrees can only be accomplished when there is a strong relationship of trust. In Peter's darkest day, sitting around the fire with the rooster about to crow, he denied Jesus three times. His flesh, worries and fear got the better of him. His former rough life of a fisherman surfaced. Interestingly, under tremendous pressure from onlookers and non-believing accusers, he did not deny the teachings of Jesus, but the person of Jesus. He distanced himself from the relationship. Actually, the relationship is what gave him eternal life. It is the relationship that opened the door to receive the words that transformed him.

In John 21 we read about the encounter when Jesus restored Peter after denying Him. What we see here is crucial. Jesus knew that going forward with Peter, whom Jesus Himself appointed as the first leader of the church, no authority, no revelation, no faithfulness and trust could be expected if the relationship was not secure and healthy.

When reading the Gospels Acts, the disciples who ran away during Jesus' crucifixion did not fully understand what was taking place. Yet, history tells us all twelve apostles travelled to distant countries to spread the Gospel – just as Jesus had commanded them. They preached with authority and power and with great conviction, and were even willing to die for their faith.

Except for the apostle John, who died of old age while imprisoned in a labour camp, all the other apostles died violent deaths as martyrs while spreading the Gospel of Jesus Christ. Some were sawn in half; pulled to pieces between horses; others boiled in hot oil; others were thrown to the lions, and some were crucified upside down.

To the twelve, the Person of Jesus was the love of God shed abroad in their hearts. This love caused them to give up their all, because they realised Jesus was worth their all. Their close relationship with Jesus transformed these twelve men into mighty warriors for the Gospel. They feared no one but God. They despised the praise of men and in their hearts, they had died to this world and all that is in it for the sake of what was worth more this world could ever offer them. This is the same conviction we find in the apostle Paul. He said he had died to this world and the world was dead to him. All he desired was to know Christ and the fellowship of His sufferings (Philippians 3:10).

It is in this close relationship that Jesus anchored His ministry which would continue powerfully after His departure – despite severe persecution and resistance from the outside world until today. This is a relational Gospel that we as believers embrace. It is not a Gospel of laws and regulations. It is a Gospel that emanates from a loving relationship with the Father, Son and Holy Spirit.

The last push

Sitting around a table with His twelve disciples, Jesus was about to celebrate the Passover meal. By now He had spent a few years telling His disciples openly that He was the Messiah, that He was the Bread of Life and the Water of Life, the Good Shepherd. He did not withhold these important truths from them. Yet He prepared to die for the sins of the world, with both Judas his betrayer and Peter the denier present in the room. Jesus took the bread and said it was His body broken for all and He lifted the cup, representing the New Covenant in His blood.

At this point, as Jesus announced His betrayal by someone in the room, He offered Judas a final chance of reconciliation. It shows us what Jesus valued the most. He values reconciliation above separation. In His Sermon on the Mount in Matthew 5-7, Jesus gave clear instructions that those who want to be His followers must demonstrate their understanding regarding the essence and value of relationships. God first, then your brother, is what Jesus taught. Maintaining a relationship requires us to turn the other check, walk the extra mile, be humble, be a peacemaker, practice marital purity, have mercy on others and maintain our 'yes' towards others. We are to love our enemies, Jesus said in Matthew 5:44, and greet those we do not know (v47). Jesus was calling for an understanding that under God we are all created and related. We are to live in such a way that we demonstrate this.

Only time will tell

We can assess how important relationships are by analysing the time we devote to human relationships compared to non-human activities, such as online, TV, news, and business deals. Our devotion should be human to human relationships and human to God. However, if we are honest, the recent developments we have seen in smartphones and the internet, have seen people interacting less and less in a personal way.

In Matthew 7:23 Jesus makes a statement that sends shivers down the spines of everyone who reads it. He sent people away from Himself who claimed to know Him, but who only did miracles in His name. This startling verse highlights the difference between true and false disciples. Jesus, speaking here in the present tense, is making a direct reference to those who have a relationship with Him while on earth. He contrasts this to those who merely used His name to perform miracles and make a name for themselves.

An impossible feat

Relationships can be very challenging to maintain and repair when needed. People can work on complex systems to solve problems, but in most cases, people shy away from working on difficulties within their relationships. Running away from or even ending a relationship might seem like a short-term solution, but most of the time this decision births long-term pain. If we are to take

God's example, He pursued peace by giving His best. When a relationship is truly important to us, we need to become personally involved in the restoration process of the person we are pursuing. This is exactly what God Himself did when Jesus pursued peace with us, His enemy. He made peace by the shedding of His own blood on the cross. No love story greater than this can ever be written.

The peace of God

In Romans 14:17 Paul describes the Kingdom, the rule and reign of God, as righteousness, peace and joy in the Holy Spirit. God's rule and reign bring forth peace, which is an attribute only God can bring. Jesus came and established that peace between God and mankind. No human feat or any amount of striving can cause the peace only God can bring. Through the sacrifice of Jesus, only God is the One who can save by forgiving and removing sin. Without the removal of sin it is an impossible feat to establish everlasting peace. This peace is an essential part of our relationship with God. The peace Jesus wrought to establish was a 'vertical peace' – a peace between God and man (Luke 2:14). This is where peace begins. Once 'vertical peace' is in place God began introducing 'horizontal peace' – peace between neighbours. Again, it is impossible for mankind to establish everlasting peace without God Himself removing the stumbling block, which is sin.

Running from ourselves

There has never been a time when mankind has been so connected and at the same time so disconnected. Modern technology and social media have made it possible for mankind to communicate twenty-four hours a day. Although people want to be connected to each other, they actually end up isolating them-selves more and more. Comparisons, online gossip, false claims and impressions created on social media and dating platforms drive wedges between people more than they connect people.

We are busier than ever before. We rest less to achieve more. We get our 'fix' quicker than those who lived at the turn of the century. The quicker the 'fix', the quicker we need another one. Mankind wants to achieve more and in doing so, we rest less. Our pursuit is to reach a place where we can rest more and be more at peace with ourselves and others.

Where the other person is coming from

To understand the other person I also need to help them under-stand me. Open and regular communication opens up channels of discussion that lead to a strong bridge being built between two parties. This bridge can carry only as much truth pushed across it during a time of intense discussion as both parties have invested in the maturing of the relationship.

Every person's background is different, and their struggles are unique. When engaging a person, it is wise to locate them first. Ask questions to establish their state of mind, together with their hidden and outright expectations.

An investment such as this, early on in a relationship, will be the medicine that heals future scars and fractures in a relationship. To understand where the other person is coming from, demonstrates a humility on your part and it honours the other person. These principles are the gems Jesus spoke about during His Sermon on the Mount (Matthew 5-7).

Did God put down the phone?

The theme throughout the Bible is God's plan to reconcile His people back to Himself. God wants His people to know Him. His desire is for His family to be with Him for eternity. Jesus' death on the cross, His burial and resurrection were all part of securing a plan of salvation to achieve the process of reconciling His people back to Himself. A reconciliation therefore points back to what once existed – a relationship. If the original relationship God had with His people had not been damaged, no reconciliation would be needed.

When a person is born again, the Spirit of God makes the person new on the inside. One of the key 'repairs' affected by the Spirit within the person, is that for the first time they can hear God communicate with them. It takes time for a believer to develop a relationship with God, and communication happens when dialogue is established. Every believer needs to study God's Word to know what He is saying and hear the voice of the Spirit. Jesus said the Holy Spirit does not speak about Himself; He reminds believers of what Jesus said and will always lead believers in the truth of God.

Why is it then after a season of hearing God, a believer experiences a perceived silence on God's part? Has God become silent or have the believer's ears become dull of hearing? What has led to the perceived silence? The worst thing in any relationship is when there is a breakdown in communication. One only must look back and find the interruption which caused the communication breakdown. When we read Genesis 3, we clearly see how disobedience acts like water on a burning fire.

On Sunday mornings churches are filled with believers who are born again, yet many of these believers, although they love God, live lives resembling their pre-salvation days. The apostle Paul addressed the church in Galatia and warned believers against a born-again life riddled with old sinful habits. His statement in Galatians 5:17 describes exactly what breaks down communication between the believer and the Spirit of God. He says the flesh wars against the Spirit of God and vice versa. This means when the believer yields to the desires and promptings of the flesh, they temporarily side with the enemy. The end result is disobedience, which leads to a downgrade of the fellowship between the believer and God. Sin is the key reason why a believer might feel as if God is absent on the other end of the phone line. Although John says in 1 John 1:8, 10 that every believer will make mistakes, He also urges the believer to correct the mistake through heartfelt repentance to restore the fellowship (1 John 1:9).

It is therefore crucial for every believer to not only be born again, but to also undergo the process of sanctification to get rid of the old sinful nature (Romans 12:2). For the believer who is willing to lay down the old life and yield to the Spirit's leading, the richest blessings and fulfilment await them eternally. They have found the way God intended for every believer, while living on earth, to develop a deep and meaningful relationship with the God of creation, the lover of our souls.

Chapter 19

What about my needs?

As humans, we live in a world where we are in constant need of assistance. We need help from others, and we are given instructions to ask our Father in heaven for help in times of need. We do not always ask our heavenly Father for help and even if we do, we do so with a slight hesitation. Not every believer can testify that God answered their prayer when they were in need. Our hesitation comes from the fact that we do not know if God will hear us or answer us when we petition Him for something.

In John 14:14 Jesus Himself said: "Ask me for anything and you shall have it." Many believers rely on this statement by Jesus, yet they read it in Scriptural isolation. Readers fail to also read Matthew 7:23: "I never knew you. Away from Me you evildoers." To understand how to ask God for help when we are in need requires that we understand how we are to ask. Jesus was explaining that discipleship is not a duty of law-observation. He wanted His listeners to understand that discipleship is more than obedient observation of the Law. Jesus' primary purpose is to re-establish relations between God and every believer. Out of this relationship voluntary obedience flows.

The title of this book hints at a layered approach, or a wheel within a wheel. Everything else flows from a healthy relationship, which is the very aspect that gives birth to obedience, to fruitfulness and growth. It is for this reason this book is titled, *Worth it all*. Our relationship with God is worth more than anything this world can offer. It is worth pursuing, because if we do not prioritise it, we will fall into the category of people to whom Jesus said: "I never knew you. Away from Me you evildoers" (Matthew 7:23).

To truly understand this, we need to go back to the history of Israel and how they, after leaving Egypt, walked through the Wilderness. Their walking through desolate terrain served to train them to rely on God for everything. Nowadays we have become so independent that it is the exception, rather than the norm, to approach God for anything. God, in rescuing His people from Egyptian slavery, initiated a relationship with Israel. This relationship, in the form a covenant, supplied all they needed. The important aspect here is the relationship that was established, plus the conditions that governed the relationship. The promises with its related conditions and the commandments received and administered by Moses, emerged from the relationship God expressed in Exodus 4:22, where He called Israel His firstborn son.

Israel's relationship with God was based on this declaration by God of Israel's sonship, which gave rise to a loving loyalty to God and Him rescuing them from slavery. This loving loyalty can also be expressed as obedience to God's commands. This is in line with the principle of a benefactor and the beneficiary. God was the benefactor to Israel and they were meant to reciprocate with their love, loyalty and faithfulness. This Old Testament principle has not changed for us who live under the New Covenant two thousand years after Christ's atonement for sin. If we forget what God has done for us, namely, He justified us by the blood of the Lamb, we forget that we need to approach God in the context of a loving relationship and reciprocal obedience.

Both the Old and New Testaments are full of God expressing His love for Jewish Israel and the Israel of God (Galatians 6:14). Jesus Himself, a full representation of the Father (Hebrews 1:3), stated in many different ways that He is looking for friends, not hirelings; sons, not slaves. He told several parables explaining that His focus was relationships, not mere functioning. His teachings testified to reconciliatory aspects. When He said: "Come unto Me, all you who are weary and burdened" (Matthew 11:28), He was again pointing back to God's role as a Father to all who would receive Him as Lord and Saviour (Matthew 11:25-27). Jesus did not say we are to return to the Law of Moses.

We approach God with our needs in the context of a relationship. What was destroyed in Genesis though the advent of sin, is what Christ came to restore, and in the last two chapters of Revelation, we read how God dwells among His people for eternity. God's desire was, is and will always be a loving relationship. When we begin to understand this, we will approach God with what we need, not what we want. We will also have full assurance of His hearing and answering us, because we will honour the relationship. Unfortunately, many Christian who have been justified, are existing apart from God, much like children who have grown up without any loving relationship with their parents. They observe a certain level of functionality when called upon, but daily loving interaction does not exist.

Risking it all

There are so many institutions teaching different faiths. Religions in this world seem like an *a la carte* menu. You choose the one that best suits your wants and desires – from appeasing all the gods because we are superstitious, to Scientology which makes a person their own saviour. There are cults, monasteries, and different branches of religion that range from mysticism to modern humanism, existentialism and many others. They are all designed to make the person feel warm and fuzzy, especially those who are anxiously searching for a meaning to this depressing life. In his book of Ecclesiastes, Solomon makes it clear that anything done without God is meaningless.

One key question remains unanswered in all these other religions: how do I know I have certainty about my passage to heaven when all of these religions have been designed and formulated by men themselves?

At which point can a person say they have attained all knowledge? What if a new set of principles are discovered? Is it not unfair to the previous generations who did not have access to them? All of this begins to resemble sinking sand – the longer you remain there the deeper you get into trouble. Your destiny is doomed. The Bible describes these as snares for the soul. All the person will find is uncertainty, disillusionment and confusion. What looked so interesting and appealing from the outside has become a snare to many seekers. Paul addressed these same questions when he discussed human wisdom in 1 Corinthians 1:18-2:16. He commented that human wisdom is unable to bring mankind to a place of knowing God – see verse 21. God's wisdom operates in such a way that it eliminates all human boasting. Paul warns us, in 1 Corinthians 2:5, against placing our faith in human wisdom.

Holding onto subjective ideologies will cause us to risk our all. Our lives will be shipwrecked like many a person who has perished with no certainty and with no clarity of their destiny. Manmade wisdom is delusional at best. It comes and goes, and it is as unpredictable as the waves of a turbulent sea. Jesus said it is the blind leading the blind. None of them provide a truly fulfilling personal relationship with our Creator. Therefore, the only certainty we have in this world is found in the Person of Christ, His Work and His Words.

A sense of security

Nothing secures a child as much as when there is a strong healthy relationship between the child and the parents. A secure child has a deep sense of 'being' and 'belonging' and therefore does not have to waste time trying to convince others of their ability. Their sense of security propels them forward and enables their talents to flourish.

What do we see in Scripture about a sense of security? When Jesus rose from the Jordan River after His baptism, His Father spoke a word of acceptance, identity and purpose to Him. Jesus never desired the praise of men like the Pharisees did (John 12:43). He knew He had the full backing of all the angelic forces in heaven to do what He was sent to do. His Sonship was secure. The close relationship in the Godhead secured His resolve.

Why do we then miss out on the position we were called to – as co-heirs with Jesus (Romans 8:17)? We are called to be Jesus' brothers and sisters in His glory, if we also share in His sufferings. Both the sufferings and glory we share with Christ fall into the framework of being relationally joined to Him. When we do understand this, we will begin to function in a different way in this world. Our relationship with God is what gives us our sense of security and identity. I would like to suggest that if our relationship with God develops to such an extent whereby we are able to do only what He asks us to do, we will find that we are less frustrated and more focused on what He has asked us to do. Our works of service will be directed by the Spirit of fellowship Himself (Acts 16:6,7). We do not perform works in order to achieve a kind of 'status' before God. We perform works of service unto God because we are joined to God in a loving relationship.

Looking up not down

Having met so many young people who struggled to relate to God, I began to draw certain conclusions from their perception of God, based on their earthly fathers. Should we draw conclusions about God as a Father based on the experiences we have had with our earthly fathers? It is my Biblical view that it would be completely wrong to do so. For us to get to know God, we need to look upwards and get a Biblical perspective for ourselves.

Harsh fathers can bring forth sons and daughters who are either themselves harsh, or their father's harshness leads them to be overcompensating parents who allow their children everything and anything. Many believers reach a stage in their relationship with God where they believe in God, they walk in holy reverence towards God, but they cannot express love. This is due to their never having received love. Generations affect generations after them and it is possible for the son or daughter to break free from a loveless father-child relationship. Once this takes place, generations to come will benefit from it. Joy will be the fruit they bear every day.

A tough one to swallow

When Jesus made the statement: "Go away from Me. I do not know you," in Matthew 7:21-23, He made it clear that entering heaven depends on more than fulfilling certain rituals. Rituals, by definition, are a series of religious actions performed according to a prescribed order. Rituals can be performed without God being present and in many cases they are performed unbeknown to the person performing the rite, as an inward-focused 'puffing up' of the flesh. Because rituals can be self-pleasing, many religious actions will not fit the description that Jesus gives of what is required before entering the Kingdom of God.

His command is not to perform many actions. Rather, Jesus points to the will of the Father as the door to the Kingdom (Matthew 7:21-23). 1 John 3:23 says the will of the Father is that we believe in Christ. In fact, we are commanded to believe in Christ. The message of Ephesians 2:8-10 is that the Holy Spirit transforms or changes Christians so that they will do good works – the believer in Christ does the will of the Father, and then the Father transforms them to become like Christ (Ephesians 4:13).

Chapter 20

Evidence of the hand of God

People may argue against the existence of God and the only proof they can offer is what science tells us. God made it clear in Romans 1:18-23 that He allows people to see the visible evidence of His creative power. God has not hidden Himself. He has made who He is clearly visible for all to see in creation and in the passion of Christ His Son who died for the sins of mankind.

God's intervention in the lives of mankind is undeniable, and the evidence of His hand is seen in the lives of people as He enters their reality throughout history. One such person is a tax collector named Zacchaeus, who was also a thief (Luke 19:8). This is an amazing account of how a person who had chased after wealth, found his identity and acceptance in God. No other power than the love of God can turn a sinful man into a free man. When Jesus stopped at the sycamore tree, Zacchaeus did not find money, wealth or status, he found a relationship with someone who accepted him. Zacchaeus experienced the Father's love, the grace of the Lord Jesus Christ, and an invitation into fellowship with the

Spirit of God. The proof of this is seen as he, later around the evening dinner table, announced that he would make recompense for all his previous wrongs. His life changed, not because he gained a worldly position, power, or money, but because he was willing to forfeit the worldly possessions he had idolised.

Zacchaeus's story is similar to that of Nicodemus, the Pharisee. This man was the 'secret believer' who visited Jesus by night (John 3:1-8). His story shows how chasing after earthly wealth faded the very moment he met Jesus. Paul makes it clear that all knowledge, all prophecy and knowing all the secrets on earth are not worth as much as love (1 Corinthians 13). Love is the expression of a relationship. 1 Corinthians 13 tells us that nothing can compare to the worth of being God's friend.

God, atheism and science

In order for any person to hold a specific philosophy or faith, there are certain key questions they have to answer for themselves. Similarly, when you are planning to enter a relationship with a person, it is wise to ask relevant questions regarding that person. This trust we place in other people, religious beliefs and or philosophies determines the direction and course of our lives.

Some of the questions we are to ask if we desire to know if God exists, for instance, include, are we mere molecules – groups of atoms bonded together, which over time, morphed into human beings with attributes like reasoning, emotions, the ability to relate and incredible creativity? Who placed a moral code inside the molecule? Is there any way we as humans have a 'greater being' looking after us? Is there anyone who accurately orders the universe to an atomic second? Are we ruled by a universal dictator? How can such an incredible universe suddenly emerge from nothing? Are we, as a species, the result of the 'big bang' and made to live on a planet with science, in our limited understanding, as our only hope of existence?

When looking at the average human being, we cannot deny the incredible feats of engineering and creativity. No other created being can match mankind's power of reasoning, planning and design. Who has 'programmed' mankind to fall in love and who designed the beautiful institution of marriage and the family? Where does all of this come from? The enormous complexities and creativity built into a single human brain demand the hand of a greater being? What is the origin of man's conscience? Are we born with a predisposition towards knowing and doing good and right, or does our moral conduct stem from a greater being, whose nature is moral and pure?

We as Christians believe in a God who is all powerful and who created everything, including mankind. We believe the God of the Bible is a loving, compassionate God who is not far off. He is present and involved in the daily lives of those who call on His name. We believe the Triune God of Scripture comprises the Father, the Son and the Holy Spirit. There are other schools of thought, apart from Christianity, that promote something other than the Triune God. One of these schools is the philosophy of deism, which believes in a greater being they call god, who is believed to be distant and removed from what he created.

Following deism removes any connection between God and mankind. This is metaphorically similar to a mother giving birth to a child and then completely abandoning that child. Individuals who follow this belief are left to their own devices and knowledge. Reason and the observation of the natural world are the guidelines to life for the deist; they believe there is a greater being out there who created them, yet this being is not interested in them. Deists are, therefore, worse off than someone who denies the existence of any God. In a deistic existence, the relationship between God and mankind doesn't exist and mankind has no hope of any external intervention or compassion when they need it. At best, the deist has a grim existence – they are never able to fully develop an identity of who they are in God, and the deistic belief renders the believer identityless, insecure, helpless, and alone.

Atheists do not believe in the existence of any God, god or greater being. Atheism bases its reasons for life and everything that exists on science, and their doctrine is the big bang theory. For the atheist, nothing created everything – there was no deity involved. Believing in the big bang theory is similar to sitting in your garden and seeing your name and surname suddenly appear, perfectly written, in the clouds. It is a philosophy that grabs whatever crumbs fall from the latest table of science. In doing so, they deny the existence of their own origin, namely God the Creator of all mankind. They also deny the amazing creative and reasoning attributes He has bestowed on all of mankind. It is interesting to see how atheism and science join hands when they try to explain the world.

Science can explain many things we see and use today. It is able to accurately predict things like the weather; it can put men on the moon and send space craft deep into space. Scientists can assist people with maternity problems, but what science cannot do, is create life. A further great inability on the part of science and atheism, is that they are unable to scientifically measure or explain love. Love, the very aspect we as humans share, is the first fruit of the Spirit of God (Galatians 5:22). Love did not originate with mankind but emanates from God. God is love and whatever He does, He does out of love. When He sent His own Son to die for the sins of the world, John 3:16 tells us God sacrificed His own because of love.

When listening to atheists presenting their case as the reason for all and Darwinism as the models we are to follow and believe, we cannot help but think that atheists do believe in a god. They deny the God of the Bible, but devote all their time, resources and energy to get everyone to believe God does not exist. Actually, the definition of worship is to show reverence or adoration to a deity or to someone of higher ranking than yourself. If atheists declare science to be the be all and end all, they have found their god.

In arguments put forward by atheists, we always hear the word they most vehemently oppose, which is 'religion'. They argue against rules, dogma, traditions and practices people have followed and embraced for millennia. But the born-again Christian does not follow a religion. They are born again by God's Spirit because of their faith in God's plan of redemption. Christianity is not a life of religious rituals and practices. It is a relationship with a loving, caring and present God.

The God Christians love, serve and worship speaks to the hearts of those who diligently seek and serve Him. His eternal Word is not a book of rules, laws and commands. Scripture is the narrative of how God planned, executed and achieved reconciliation with the one created in His image on earth. The Bible is a love story with guidelines on how to remain in the eternal relationship God is offering all of mankind.

In many cases, people who have never experienced true love are more prone to deny giving or receiving love. Atheism at its core denies, not only the existence of God, but the existence of a loving God. If not for the love of God, no meaningful relationships could ever exist, both in heaven and on earth. Denying the existence of God is to deny the attributes and actions related to love in any shape or form. What atheists cannot explain is that they all live in a society where love is visible and tangible, yet they deny love, which is a reminder of what God created in the Garden of Eden.

History is littered with people who, using their God-given reasoning, argue against the existence of God. The apostle Paul was confronted by such men. His statement to them still silences all arguments against the existence of God. Paul stated that God showed his invisible attributes in and through creation (Romans 1:19-20). He did this so that no person will have an excuse on the day of reckoning. To see the greatness of God, we only have to pause and observe the incredible accuracy with which the universe has been created and has been sustained. If, according to science and atheism, the universe has been in existence for billions of years, who or what has kept it in such perfect balance for so long, and how and why? Cosmologists call this the 'fine-tuning of the universe'. Another example of evidence for the existence of God is man's creative designing and achievements throughout history. The greatness of God demands that we not only acknowledge His existence, but pay the necessary respect, awe and worship to God. He is more than just a greater being. He is our Lord and Saviour.

We should ask ourselves why there is destruction in our world. We should investigate who is responsible for so many lives lost daily. If we do, we will find that the devil is at work in the world. Because of people's ignorance, God, in many cases, gets labelled with the devil's handywork. People are quick to deny the existence of God, but they fail to explain the existence of evil. If, in the atheistic worldview, God does not exist, then no other being, other than humans, ought to exist – nor God not the devil. Who then is to blame for anarchy and destruction?

One of the atheist's main arguments against the existence of God is that God did not create man – their claim is that it is man who created 'God'. Christians can testify to the personal relationship they have with God, but on a grander scale, you first need to prove the existence of God. To assist the believer in knowing and trusting in the God who created mankind and the entire universe, I have included a few brief arguments for the existence of God:

Teleological argument

This is the argument for the existence of God from the evidence of order and fine-tuning of the universe and nature. Planets' orbit, time and space are in perfect order since they were created.

Ontological argument

The argument that God, being defined as most great or perfect, must exist since a God who exists is greater than a God who does not.

Moral argument

The fact that we as humans order ourselves by means of a divinely given set of rules.

Factual argument

Actual documented history of Jesus' existence, His grave, the resurrection and His documented appearance to hundreds of people simultaneously. From Old to New Testament documented history cannot be denied (Romans 1:20-22).

Cosmological argument

An argument for the existence of God that claims that all things in nature depend on something else for their existence (that is, they are contingent), and that the whole cosmos must therefore itself depend on a being that exists independently or necessarily. As part of the Cosmological argument, the Kalan Cosmological argument is worth mentioning. It refutes the atheistic claim that God does not exist. If the atheist's main argument is based on science, then let science itself refute their claim that God does not exist. Contrary to the big bang theory being responsible for all life and expansion, the universe cannot cause itself. Its cause must therefore exist beyond the space-time universe. This cause must be spaceless, timeless, immaterial, uncaused, unimaginably powerful … well, it must be like God. The cosmological argument therefore shows that it is quite reasonable to believe that God exists.

No matter how wicked this world could become; no matter how distant people can grow from God; there will always be a remnant of those who will exemplify the love of God. Science has no formula or explanation for love. Love can be explained and embodied in many different ways.

There is a love deeper than just the love we as humans are familiar with. This is a love that transcends human minds. It is not the love for our close family, nor the love for one's good-hearted neighbour. The love that silences scientists and atheists, is the love for those who hate and hurt us. It is a love that forgives; that is unconditional. It is the love of God. It is a love that is stronger than offence – it admits wrongdoing but goes beyond the wrong and provides for a forgiveness to undo the wrong.

Atheists argue against the existence of God and put science in the place of God. Their argument is flawed in that a loving God is replaced by a knowledge-based god. Science, they argue, grows, and develops and in so doing gives us the ability to know and do more. But science is not the key to the mysteries of life. It cannot generate, understand, quantify nor replicate love. Love did not originate in science nor was it engineered by mankind. Love, as Scripture explains it, is the key attribute of God. No matter how an atheist tries to argue against the existence of God, they still look after their children and kiss them goodbye in the mornings when they leave for school. The loudest advocate for atheism is often the one who is most desperate for attention and affection, whether as a result of childhood or other experiences. I deal with the subject of acceptance, attention-seeking and other related issues later in this book.

Atheism cannot explain the love a human is able to show in the face of anger and hatred. It is more than mere affection we can also observe in animals. This love is something that can only come from a loving God. Salvation, as described in John 3:16, is us responding to God's love. God's love is unconditional; it reaches out to us apart from any good or bad works we have done. Science has no category for the love God shows us, nor does it have any explanation for the love a human is able to show to its enemies. This is not a love they have generated from within them-selves – it is received from God as a sign that the love of God is shed abroad in their hearts.

In 1 Corinthians 8:1-3, Paul says there is a clear difference between knowledge and love. In his own words, according to the

NIV: "Knowledge puffs up while love builds up." Paul's explanation of love in 1 Corinthians 13 says love is humble, not self-seeking, not boastful. He says love always trusts, perseveres and hopes. These are the trademarks of a relationship.

We know that love cannot exist outside the boundaries of a relationship. Love is what empowers us. Through love, God calls, commissions and directs our ways. Our loving relationship with God is our strength, because it not only connects us to God, it teaches us who God is, what He is like, and how God operates. If you want to enter into a relationship with God, just read John 3:16.

Knowledge, on the other hand, makes people self-assertive and independent. It develops within people a self-styled authoritarian attitude of always 'knowing better'. Knowledge, if it becomes a person's source of trust and identity, will drive them away from God. It is the 'carrot' Satan dangled in front of Adam and Eve in the Garden of Eden. The Tree of Knowledge of Good and Evil births within a person a knowledge-based independence. It destroys the relationship they have with God.

Is all knowledge wrong? Not at all. God encourages us to grow in the knowledge of Him to get to know Him better. What He does not encourage us to do, is to pursue knowledge as an end to enlightenment. Knowledge without a relationship with God can overtake our lives and make us unteachable and arrogant. Science is where most atheists hang their coats. Their arguments and reasoning are all based on scientific knowledge. If science cannot explain something, they refuse to accept it. Well, this is the very reason why they persistently argue against the existence of God. God is love and science cannot explain love.

I recently heard an atheist state that the premise of Luke 16:19-31, where the rich man and Lazarus die and open their eyes in their respective destinations of choice, was absolute rubbish. His theory was that to the atheist, death is similar to falling asleep. One moment you are awake and the next moment you are asleep. When you fall asleep you lay down all plans, power, influence, ideologies, knowledge and you disappear into the dark abyss. His theory is that in death you cease to exist. But if we are destined for a demise with nothing to live for, nothing to aspire towards, and no lasting friendships, what is the point of living? Why should we establish ourselves in careers and aim towards improvement in something that will inevitably cease to exist? Why should we even pay attention to our diet and what we say and do? Why should we pay any attention to any sort of moral code? Why do we celebrate families and the birth of a child? Why do we mourn the death of a loved one? Should we not just live our lives the way we want to and then disappear? Is there no reason for disciplining the flesh, aspiring to maintain the moral high ground and continuous faithfulness to God despite hardships? Why give our lives to any cause if 'all is vanity'?

Those purporting atheism and no life after death, should read Ecclesiastes where Solomon comes to the conclusion that whatever we do without God, which he describes as "under the sun" is meaningless, vanity and void of any fulfilment. The wisest man who ever lived gave us his closing remark: "Fear God and keep His commandments, for this is the whole duty of man" (Ecclesiastes 12:13 NIV). If mankind's greatest achievements are done without them being founded on their relationship with the eternal God, they remain meaningless. No matter the fervour with which atheists argue against a mountain of truth, it makes no difference to a person's eternal destiny if they do not believe in God or life after death. The arguments for the existence of God, spelt out above, are the very proof that will judge mankind on the day of reckoning (Romans 1:19-20).

A personal perspective

I overheard an apologetic pastor conversing with a non-believer who did not believe in life after death. The pastor said: "What if I allow God to save me, to plan my life, to direct my steps and I personally take responsibility for my diet and conduct. In doing so I have lived a good healthy life. If, when I die, there is no God, then I have not lost anything at all. But what if God exists and He rewards me with eternal rewards for a life lived according to His commands – in that case I have gained it all. Now, consider the opposite. What if I live an unhealthy, meaningless life, pay no attention to any moral laws and lived without any purpose or sense of direction. If, when I die and there is no God, I will cease to exist. But if I die and God exists, then I have lost it all."

My most important reason

My single most important reason why it is worth my all to serve, follow and worship God, is when I stand under the starry sky at night, I cannot help thinking that someone greater than me created this and me. Someone greater than the Milky Way created the universe. The most amazing though is that the 'Some-one' who created all of this, accepts me as His son. He wants to know me and wants me to know Him. He wants to live in my heart and help me shake off the rottenness of this broken world so that I can co-exist with Him forever. The number of my prayers He has answered, the number of times He has protected me, the hope and reassurance I have in His Word and the billions of people, the great cloud of witnesses, who also put their trust in God, they all inspire me to run my race to the end. God is truly worth it all. He is worth my all.

Scientists, agnostics, and many atheists still battle with the same question the Pharisees did in Jesus' time. They cannot understand how and why God would become a man who dies a shameful death to be a sacrifice for mankind's sin? The reason for this is because they use their own broken earthly relationship as the standard to evaluate who God is, what He has said and done.

Part Six

Working and walking

Chapter 21

The crucial balance

I f we look at how God structured His friendship with Adam, it would be helpful to structure our lives in a similar way. In Genesis 2:15-17, God created the Garden of Eden and put man in it to work it. The job description was to work it and take care of it, and it came with a command: "You are free to eat from any tree in the garden, but you must not eat from the tree of the knowledge of good and evil, for when you eat from it you will surely die." God's work came with God's commands. We see this pattern in the life of Adam, in the lives of Israel and in the New Testament church. To Adam it was work and take care of your environment, and walk in obedience. To Israel it was to uphold the rituals and ceremonial practices God gave through Moses. Their lives had to show an obedience to the Lord's commands to be a light to the nations around them, to remain holy and to reveal God's nature and character. To the New Testament church, the calling of God has not changed. We are called to be a royal priesthood, a holy nation, God's special possession that declares the praises of Him who called us out of darkness. Part of us being the New Israel (Galatians 6:16) requires that we do the work entrusted to us: "Go and make disciples of all nations" (Matthew 28:19). Since creation God has given His people work to do.

However, when we look at Genesis 2, we see how God walked with Adam. Adam was with God when he named the animals, the birds and beast in the field. Even in chapter 3, after Adam fell into sin, God walked in the garden where Adam was. God was looking for His friend. He gave mankind certain work to do, and from Genesis 2, to this day, this has not changed. We also see that God walked with Adam, which reminds us that work should not prevent us from walking with Him. Working and walking should be a crucial balance as God demonstrated in the first seven days of creation. Instead of 'working for God' we should focus on 'walking with God'. If our walking becomes a priority, our working will be blessed and pleasing to God. It will unlock the rest God demonstrated in Genesis 2:2.

Genesis 3 is a demonstration of what happens when we neglect walking with God. Walking with God represents our relationship with God and is the road that gives us direction in life to accomplish what God has given us to do – nothing more and nothing less. When this umbilical cord is severed, working gets the better of us. We get distracted and take our eyes off God, we fall into temptation and allow strange ideas to distract us. Eventually we walk away from God to another master.

God gave Adam work and regulations governing that work. It was a working relationship based on trust. Walking with God is where trust is built that enhances our working for God. In Jesus' parable of the talents (Matthew 25:30), the master entrusted work to people he was in a relationship with. In this relationship, trust ensured an increase for both the servant and the master. In verses

26-27 we clearly see what a lack of trust accomplishes. Here the master did not lose but the servant did. True working is only possible within a healthy relationship where trust is present.

Working and walking requires a crucial balance, as demonstrated from the beginning of man's existence. Unfortunately we have perfected the art of working ourselves to a standstill. We work first and then allocate time we have left to God. God did not call us to work only – this would equate to slavery and not the friendship God speaks of throughout Scripture. A relationship based purely on blind working obedience is what all other religions in this word are founded on. From Buddhism, to Scientology, to ancestral worship, they all lack the one main aspect found only in Scripture – working and walking. We are to work, and at the same time walk with the Triune God Who is alive and living in us in a sacred bond. It is a humble friendship and a divine mystery, as described by both Paul and Peter.

In the life of every person the sun sets every day. We fall into bed, tired from what we have created and the demands of this world – in fact we are drained by a master in this world, who, by his own admission in Job 1:7, is a restless, hard-working person who is self-consumed.

Scripture begins with work and rest. God worked and then rested. As Christians, we have been given six days to work and a day of rest to fellowship with God. Rest is both physical and spiritual. Working can become a lifestyle that keeps us so busy that we cannot rest to hear God's voice. It can become a vicious circle where we only realise too late we have become addicted to working and not walking. Our surprise will turn to bitter regret when we, towards the end of our lives, realise we have not entered God's rest. We have been so busy and we have not developed a friendship with Him. Focusing on working to achieve greatness, we become a friend of the world and an enemy of God (James 4:1-4). If we understand this working and walking, we will be empowered with wisdom from God's Spirit to structure our lives in such a way as to ensure our occupations, our desires and what we dream of possessing will not encroach on our walk with God. All our striving in this life for this life ends in this life. Our working serves as part of our fellowship with God. But be warned: we easily forget the One who wants to walk with us. Time spent in the service of the King is not the same as time spent in the presence of the King. We need to allow the Spirit of fellowship to guide us to maintain this balance.

A work-only life is a harsh existence with ever-moving goalposts. It is empty and void of any true fulfilment. On the other hand, a walk-only life delivers no increase in God's investment in us. We as the workers will also suffer when, to our great disappointment, we receive no crown as a reward on the great day of reckoning.

Lastly, walking with God enhances our working with and for God. The closer we walk with God, the clearer will be our communication with the Father, Son and Holy Spirit. If the Holy Spirit could stop Paul from spreading the Gospel in the province of Asia (Acts 16:6-7), then we can also have Him lead us by tuning our ears to His voice. In doing this, we will truly bless the Father when we do only the work He wants us to do (see Jesus' statements in John 5:19 and John 14:10).

Doing only the work God has called us to do will release His blessing and we will show forth fruitfulness. His divine peace will guide our hearts and minds and keep us from coveting the work done by others. The aim is clear, direct and reliable communication, which makes it easier to distinguish the correct work to do.

Some work might seem right for us, but God did not call us to it. In many cases Christians make the mistake of pursuing work out of a sense of guilt or selfish ambition, which can cause them to drift away from God. They might even resist what the Holy Spirit is doing or wants to do.

A lot of Christian work might appear noble, and we might even feel called to it, but we could end up busying ourselves with something someone else was called to do. The danger when we work and do not walk is that we could become like the Pharisees in Jesus' time. They lost their connection with God and used the Law, the very thing God gave to His people, to murder Jesus. Jesus even corrected them in John 5:36 when He said that the works He does would testify about His relationship with His Father. In verses 39-40 Jesus said their diligent work and studying cannot replace the relationship Ged desires for them. They made the Law their final goal and in doing so excluded God from their lives. God is love, yet their lives show everything but love. Because relational love was missing, their whole outlook had changed from that of caring shepherds, to leaders who abused, killed and maimed God's sheep. Despite their knowledge, they remained empty on the inside. They had lost the most important thing in life, which is their relationship with God, and because of this, they became obsessed with enforcing a harsh obedient observance of the Law. To them this meant "doing good works". They were incapable of giving or receiving love because of the absence of a relationship with the God of love.

If we are not careful, we could end up like those Pharisees who were unknowingly fighting God. They were approving what God disapproved of and were denouncing what He announced.

Not hearing God's heart means we have to rely on our own instincts, our assumptions and biased information. Jesus says in verses John 5:17-23 He and His Father are working to this day. In one sentence, Jesus made it clear why the Pharisees are in the dark. Unlike them, His relationship with His Father in heaven was what guided Him; it was the very essence of everything Jesus said and did. There are so many things He could have done, yet He only did what His Father asked Him to do. Jesus expressed the heart of love, which is relational obedience. He walked with and worked with His Father. Works of this nature are worth more than all the wealth in this world.

What artists say through songs

On a personal note, I have for many years pondered the origin and practice of modern-day popular music. Music has the ability to speak to nations across many boundaries. It originated with God, despite its perversions in today's world. I have found it interesting that almost all popular songs written and sung are either about an author's desire for a relationship, the end of a relationship, or about a troubled relationship. In most cases in secular music, the so-called 'love' they sing about is distorted, and in most cases it is more about lust rather than the true love God designed it to be.

In recognising how few songs are written about non-relational matters, we can see how mankind uses the medium of music to express their sorrow regarding broken relationships. Those who write and sing these songs are predominantly singing about their human relationships. As said previously, relationships originated from God. If the expressed desire for human to human relationships dominate our secular music, why is it that mankind refuses to acknowledge their need for a relationship with their heavenly Father?

As the author I would like to challenge every reader of this book to ponder the songs written over the last sixty years, and notice that relationships feature in the lyrics of songs and song titles. It shows that even in man's fallen state, they cannot distance themselves from the powerful desire God has placed within them to be connected relationally with their fellowman and with God. People might not be saying directly that they desire relationships, but they say it indirectly in songs.

We cannot do without

As Christians, our lives should be built around God's presence and His ways, similar to how the Old Testament Israel's whole existence centred on God's presence and the tabernacle. Once a believer has built a relationship with the God who saves and indwells, they cannot do without it. God is our faithful best friend. The relationship we have with Him by the Holy Spirit, the Spirit of fellowship, is our solid ground, our secure footing, our constant in an ever-changing world, our anchor in the sea of our emotions. God is our discernment in a world of false prophets and confusing options, our harbour away from a stormy sea, and the godly wisdom in our decision-making. He is the power to accomplish His call. God, by His Holy Spirit, is our closest companion and helper. He sticks closer than a brother and is our intimate helper, the quiet voice of reason in a time of need.

In a broken world, why would any believer want to go without the guidance and stability of God's Spirit? To go without the Spirit is to lose the holiness of God. To lose the Spirit's friendship is to fall away from God's divine presence. It spells a life-journey ending in guaranteed disaster. The Spirit of God as our closest companion is easily grieved and we, as in any other relationship, need to ensure we honour Him at all times. He has been sent to us as our Helper – someone we did not deserve to receive. He is also someone Who should not be taken for granted. The Spirit is God Himself indwelling us. He is a sensitive person and not a powerful force. Seeing the Spirit of God as a force only, is similar to making a friend with the sole aim of benefiting from his or her resources. It borders on abuse and dishonesty.

How can we describe our relationship with the eternal Spirit of God? The relationship we have with the Spirit is similar to the sensitive relationship found in marriage. It is a friendship where mistakes or misunderstandings will take place – as in any close friendship. When one of the spouses in a marriage hurts the other, the trust within their relationship is broken and eventually the relationship can be permanently lost. Our relationship with the Spirit of God is similar. Scripture warns believers against wounding the Spirit and breaking trust (Mark 3:28-30 and Hebrews 6:4-6). When we get saved, we enter into a relationship with God by His indwelling Spirit. Within the context of any relationship, the most important aspect is trust. Should this crucial element be violated, like adultery in a marriage, it brings forth the most incredible pain, regret and suffering. In many cases the relationship cannot be restored.

Through our relationship with God's Spirit, we not only gain the intimate friendship of God, we also receive wisdom, love and life. Without God's Spirit we are totally lost like a ship without an anchor – drifting towards the rocks. God's Spirit is our best friend and is someone we cannot do without.

David was Israel's most prominent king and he possessed extraordinary talents. He was known for fighting wars, for designing the temple his son Solomon later built, for being a fearless shepherd, who, at a young age, killed lions and bears. It was during his younger days that he learnt to walk with God and penned poetry to worship God. Not only was he known for his victories, but he was also known for his mistakes. David committed adultery and murder.

When David was confronted by the prophet Nathan, he expressed deep regret and sorrow for his mistake, and he uttered an interesting request in Psalms 51:11. He asked God not to cast him away from His presence, nor take His Holy Spirit from him. It was not common for an Old Testament person to possess the Spirit of God as David did. It is believed by many that David had what is called, "a secret anointing." Very few people in the Old Testament had the same closeness to the Holy Spirit as David did. He knew his mistake with Bathsheba risked his close friendship with God's Spirit. Since he was young, David knew the powerful presence of God and what it would mean should the Spirit of God depart from Him. He understood the impact sin had on his relationship with God – his adultery and murder meant breaking the special trust he had with God's Spirit. Both his incredible walk with God and his mistakes teach us that we are fallible and demonstrate that God receives us back into fellowship when we truly repent for our mistakes.

We sometimes do not consider the evidence of the Spirit's presence in the life of a person like David. He wrote many of the Psalms in Scripture, and the outflow of the Spirit's presence in David's life was visible in the richness of his worship. David's son Solomon's life also demonstrated incredible wisdom through the infilling of the Spirit of God. The feats of engineering, administration and wisdom literature he penned were undeniable evidence of God's Spirit present in him. It is noteworthy that both David and Solomon were not without mistakes before God, but despite their weaknesses, their intimate walk with the Spirit of God remains something to be desired by every believer today.

David's amazing story of a real-life Biblical figure who shared an intimate friendship with God, shows us that having God's Spirit as our intimate friend is worth it all.

Chapter 22

Beware of pitfalls

E arlier in the book I discussed why it sometimes seems as if God is distant and silent. When considering the importance of the relationships we have with God and each other, there are several aspects we need to take note of. Some of the things mentioned here are for us to consider or avoid in order to improve our relationships.

How quickly 'self' creeps in

I have noticed in church circles that very few people know what the meta-narrative, the main theme of the Bible, actually is. When I did a Q&A about the purpose of Scripture, some students gave rather interesting answers while others remained silent. It is my theological view that the purpose of Scripture is to tell us more about God and teach us to glorify Him. I also hold the view that the meta-narrative in Scripture is 'Reconciliation' – I believe it is God's aim to restore the broken relationship between Himself and mankind through His plan of redemption, which is the Person and work of Christ.

I have seen that when believers do not know either the meta-narrative or the purpose of Scripture, a self-centred approach develops in their faith. The rotten "self" slips in and Christianity becomes a monologue. Such believers harvest from Scripture what they need and don't allow the Spirit of God, the true Author of Scripture, to reveal what He wants to say. Without the meta-narrative and the purpose of Scripture as a roadmap in their walk to spiritual maturity, they remain like babes in the faith. All they embrace is, 'Freedom from Egyptian slavery,' – they have been justified by grace through faith and that is all they know, all they have, and all they assume they need. Such believers begin to view God as their go-to-super-Being who is out there somewhere to provide all their needs and wants. In their thinking and through wrong teachings, God is on stand-by, ready to be at their beck and call, and even portrayed as someone who will provide a shoulder to cry on.

This wrong perception of God makes Him appear like a parent who gave up His children for adoption and is distant and uninvolved in their lives. Such a view of God develops a mindset that God is like a vending machine. In reality, the opposite is true. God Himself uses the image of a bride in marriage when He describes believers. Both the Old and New Testaments instruct us this way. Marriage is all about a relationship – in this case an eternal friendship with God. God also proclaims that He is the Great Shepherd, the lover of our souls, the father who welcomes the prodigal son, the one who cries over the ignorance of His people, the Husband of an unfaithful wife, and the One who dwells and walks with us. These beautiful images that God Himself painted for us, nullify self-centred perceptions about God.

Why do unhelpful perceptions about God persist in believing communities? Many young believers have not been taken through the process of discipleship, and they fail to develop independently in their walk with God. Other believers fail in their personal responsibility to pray, to read and to study God's eternal Word.

There are two very simple, yet powerful corrective steps to re-align a believer's ignorant misunderstanding about God. First, we are to understand that Christianity requires us not only to believe, but also behave. Believing in Christ must be followed by behaving like Him. Second, we all are to cultivate a thankful heart ready to receive and give back, a humble heart full of appreciation. Such is a fertile heart. In Matthew 5, Jesus calls it a contrite or soft heart. If we do this, our lives will resemble a garden rich with fertile soil in which the Gardener can plant His seed for a bumper harvest all year round. The condition of our garden will reflect our relationship with God.

Character issues

Character issues can make or break any relationship. In our developmental stages we are little sponges of what we see, hear and experience. But as we grow older we find we have our own opinions, we like and dislike some things, and we have an inward or outward persona. So where do we start changing and how do we streamline ourselves to forge healthy relationships and maintain the ones we are in? We cannot change what and who we are. We did not choose our environment, our culture, nor were we asked which positive and negative experiences we would like to have.

What we can do is invite and allow the Spirit of God to sanctify us. Scripture calls Him our Helper and so let us allow Him to do the work He is willing and able to do within us. He has been sent to develop Christlikeness in us. Where there is more than one person, opinions will differ, and friction will arise. That is a how God created us – no two people are identical. When the Spirit of God helps us with our character issues, we can bring much more love into a relationship rather than friction, inflexibility and disunity. Scripture calls Him the Spirit of fellowship and we will do well to allow Him to help us in our relationships. In Jesus' Sermon on the Mount, He advocates that in a relationship we are to seek the good of others, not to gather worldly assets in return for eternal rewards and to be willing to be the least. The Spirit's influence and input in our lives will help us build healthy relationships with those around us, and will also fully develop our relationship with God. He will bring us to the place where John the Baptist cried out, "He must become more; I must become less" (John 3:30).

What to avoid

Relationships are never easy to maintain, especially when there are more than two people involved. When religion is thrown into the mix, things can get even more complex. In many cases, religion brings harsh rules and associated penalties, and it can bring inflexibility in people's ideologies and worldviews. It tends to isolate people from the outside world. Defined as a pursuit followed with great devotion, it is also described as a system of faith and worship. Based on definitions, religion is evidently an expression from within a person to reach out and glorify someone greater than themselves. It is a fact that mankind, as created by God, will always display some sort of yearning to worship a greater being – someone they can look up to, ask for advice and assistance, because of the hunger God has placed within the heart of man. God has linked Himself to mankind forever. It is a beautiful and unbreakable bond. Both mankind and the devil have attempted to question and remove this bond, but there will never be anything that can fill man's longing to be relationally connected to God Himself.

Unfortunately, religion has the potential to turn its outward focus to an inward focus. Instead of focusing on the greater Being out there, mankind looks inward to try and perfect themselves, based on their own terms and conditions. When this happens, pride slips in. The flesh boasts when it fulfils a set of rules or laws. The focus on the external greater Being is lost and self-righteousness ends up being the driving force. Hard work, personal devotion and sacrifices are seen as the steps towards perfection. What this 'perfection' looks like, no one is sure. Scripture tells us Christlikeness should be our goal, but to achieve this, we are taught how to lay down our self-efforts.

Interestingly, religion can be achieved by a person on their own, and religious pursuits can be exercised without the need for love, which is the key element of a relationship with God. Their own rules guide them – similar to the blind leading the blind – and is a monologue that requires no relationship. Religion can become a cold performing of ceremonial acts, in which no love is given or received.

Christianity is the only way mankind can be joined to God in a deep, loving, and personal way. Scripture depicts this relationship as the institution of marriage as God intended it, incorporating births, love, trust, respect, servanthood, purpose, destiny, provision, and protection.

Religion has the potential to stifle relationships. Depending on the religious belief followed, the elevation of function over loving relational dependency is taught. Religion often imposes rigidity over flexibility and self-centredness over mutual benefit. In many cases the promotion of harsh treatment of the flesh seems appealing and even cleansing, but remains unable to permanently cleanse a person from within. Self-fulfilled religious beliefs and practices are the opposite of what God intended through Christianity – which has as its main goal a deep meaningful relationship with God Himself. Should we decide to pursue religion and its accompanying rituals as a way of reaching God, we will find that God becomes distant and silent, and we could perceive Him as harsh. Because there is no relationship with God, we will persistently work harder, striving for His approval and acceptance.

The enemy of relationships

In relationships, an element exists that has the capacity to cause its downfall. It hides within the inner counsel of both humans and angelic beings and is the reason God removed Adam and Eve from His holy presence. It is the reason why mankind is still running from God. This element is sin, and it has the ability to destroy any relationship.

Everything God does is relationally rooted, and it is for this reason that even the earth has to be newly created because of the entrance of sin. Man was given rule and reign over the earth and when they fell into sin, everything was affected by God's judgement (Genesis 3:17).

Where does sin come from? Scripture explains how pride was found in Lucifer (Ezekiel 28:11-15). His treasonous act of rebellion was so staggering, it even caused war in heaven (Revelation 12:7-9). There can be no greater breakdown in any relationships than for someone to make war against the God of love. Lucifer's heart grew proud because of his beauty and position as the guardian cherub. He wanted to be like God, which was also the issue he used to tempt Adam and Eve (Genesis 3:5). Lucifer's selfish ambition was to elevate himself above God, and his pursuits were driven by pride. Eventually his ambition caused the breakup of the relationship between himself and God. This rebellious action, introduced by the lies of Satan, was duplicated in Adam and Eve when they disobeyed God and attempted to be like God. It led to the breakdown of relations between God and man and man and man. The relational breakdown caused by Lucifer in heaven, and the eventual fallout seen in the actions of mankind, was so great and in such need of restoration, that the blood of Jesus was needed, firstly to purify the heavenly temple (Hebrews 9:23), and thereafter to atone for mankind's sin (Hebrews 10:12-14).

Sin gives birth to pride, which produces self-absorbed ambition. These in turn blind the individual, who begins to walk in presumption and arrogance. The enemy of any relationship reveals itself as pride. The hidden agenda of pride is self-centredness, which becomes evident when a person begins to believe their own lies. Self-centredness leads to unfaithfulness, broken trust and immense hurt – these are the rewards of sin, which always drive away love. Sin promotes me-first and it disregards truth and logic. It opposes authority, it takes but never gives, it promotes disunity, it produces strife, and it wars against peace. It resists the Holy Spirit, described in Scripture as the Spirit of fellowship. At the core of selfish pride, we find a self-centred opinionated person who is in it for themselves. It is the opposite of the very nature and definition of what a relationship is.

Pride always foolishly promotes 'self' at all costs. The essence of pride and the pursuit of what pride offers, are irrational because pride did not originate with God, which means it cannot bring righteousness, peace and joy. It can never fulfil its promises, because it blinds people to the historical results of what happened to Lucifer. Pride re-programmes a person's thinking to presumptuously set their own boundaries and develop their own wisdom. The end result is destruction and the loss of friendships and love.

Pride destroys all unity, trust and progress. Like acid, selfishness corrodes any relationship. People might enter into relationships with pure motives, but circumstances might change and self-centredness surfaces. At this point, the selfish person and the relationship they are involved in decline.

God wants us to depend on Him for all we need. A healthy dependency within a relationship is a sign of a healthy relationship – it is the opposite to selfishness or independence caused by self-centredness.

God called Gideon to demolish the idols Israel had built because those idols were a testimony of Israel's departure from their relationship with God. After Gideon destroyed the idols, God called the nation to fight the enormous Midianite-army. God wanted to demonstrate to Israel that if they put Him first, He would fight their battles with and for them. In Judges 7:2, God said pride would overtake the people if they themselves fought against the Midianites. He reduced their army to only three hundred men to get rid of any pride and independence.

One of the greatest sins mankind commits daily, is their drive towards independency from God. It stems from a sense of self-centredness, which eventually develops into living in the wrong expectation that 'self' can achieve righteousness apart from the cross of Jesus Christ.

Another way sin is expressed in mankind's actions is when people are more drawn to the world and what it offers them, than they are drawn to God. John explains this in 1 John 2:15-17 when he says people who "love" this world and all it offers subconsciously express a hatred towards God. The fall of man, which brought sin into the world, is a direct result of Satan deceiving mankind to commit sin. This world is full of darkness and John expresses it as the desires of the flesh and the boastful pride of life (1 John 2:15-17). He says these attributes found in the world are not of God the Father and do not relate to love. They are from another father – the father of lies. If a person is drawn into the pursuit of what the world offers, they will be in direct conflict with God's nature and will for mankind.

Jesus made it clear in John 17:16 that those who believe in Him are in this world but not of it. Sin drives this world and its pursuits, which is why God has to recreate this world. Loving this world prevents us from developing a relationship with God. A love for this world embodies a life of sin, which John says, prevents us from having a true relationship with God. In 1 John 2:15-17, we see that an affinity for the world is sin, which is expressed as hatred towards God. The opposite is also true. If we resist the temptations offered by this world, we respond to the love God has shown to all of humanity.

What fasting can expose

During a recent time of fasting at our church, I asked our congregation what they most missed – eating, drinking or doing. A few people said they missed a certain type of food or beverage. Others said they really struggled to make time for prayer. Some even said they became aggressive and grumpy. Many said they went through stages of emotional ups and downs. One aspect that caught my attention was the impact on people's relationships. Fasting brought people together as they began to realise they had been living selfish lives. For others, fasting also pushed people apart as their cravings caused them to become aggressive and short-tempered with each other.

In light of this, I ask a question. If we look at our busy lives and how we need coping mechanisms to survive, how much more do we neglect time with God? Fasting food or an activity makes us realise that, although we do need them, we have allowed them to become the centre of our lives. If we do not have access to these items or activities, we become upset and feel emotionally sick – we turn our backs on God and fill our lives with fleshly cravings. We busied our lives to such an extent that we cannot spend time with God.

During a fast we experience cravings and we live through an emotional roller-coaster. Can these experiences be an indication of something bigger – of our bodies crying out for something it needs? Now imagine how our spirits cry out when they are deprived of the presence of God. David expressed this anguish when he cried out to God in Psalm 51:11 to not take His Spirit from him. David understood what it would be like if God withdrew from him.

Fasting exposes things we do not need and at the same time it focuses on the one thing we do need. Setting aside worldly desires and activities force us to evaluate how God sees us. Saying no to worldly pursuits brings us back to the place where we realise our dependency on God. It helps us rekindle our love for God and we step back into fulfilling our God-intended purpose, which is walking closely with God. We realise that it is worth it all to set aside worldly pleasures and focus more of our time and energy on developing our relationship with Him.

Part Seven

Worth it all

Chapter 23

How to deepen and grow relationships

G od exists in the relationship we know as the Trinity. From this we learn in Genesis 1 how He created mankind not only to exist in and through a relationship with Him, but also with each other. The Bible reveals God's love. In Scripture, we see how God's love-nature is expressed as a giving God. He gives as He creates and sustains. He gives rain to all – the righteous and the unrighteous. He gives talents and gifts to people.

Although many never acknowledge God as the source of their creativity, they still display the greatness of God.

Jesus hanging on a cross was God's ultimate demonstration of His love through the greatest gift of life to all humanity. John 3:16 describes this: "For God so loved the world that He gave His one and only Son, that whoever believes in Him shall not perish but have eternal life" (NIV). God gave Himself to reconcile humanity back to Himself by extending a hand of friendship towards a rebellious people who were created to be His family.

God provided for His people during their journey from Egyptian slavery throughout their Wilderness wanderings until they settled in the Promised Land, God not only provided all they needed by giving them food, shelter, guidance, protection, He also gave them Himself by being present with them. If we are looking for a way to deepen and grow our own relationship with God and others, we should adopt the heart as God.

We can ask ourselves what a 'giver' looks like. A giving God gives us what we need, He is always accessible to us. Giving is far more than just handing out gifts. From a Biblical perspective, giving can be described as someone who has a concern for someone else. Such a person will invest time to see that the other person's needs are met, that they are cared for and protected, that their future is secure, and that they be with each other, which requires time and effort and a prioritising of resources. Giving of yourself is a heart-felt demonstration of love and it requires that we do the same as God. He gave His best. He did not send an angel but came to earth in person to die for a sinful world.

In Luke 6:38 Jesus said: "Give and it will be given to you." Paul makes a similar statement in Acts 20:35 during his farewell to the Ephesian elders when quoting Jesus: "It is more blessed to give than to receive." It appears from their words that giving is a principle God looks for and rewards.

The act of giving has two important aspects to it.

First, it removes selfishness and self-centredness from a relationship. A relationship creates an environment in which others are nurtured and developed. Marriage is a safe place for intimacy where spouses give to each other themselves in an environment of vulnerability. When selfishness enters a relationship, giving is quickly replaced by demanding. A mutual building of one another is turned into a destruction of each other. If God is love and expresses Himself by being a giver of gifts, then Satan is the opposite. He is totally selfish and self-centred. His whole outlook is taking, not giving, destroying, not growing.

Second, giving develops the giver and it purifies the receiver. In Ephesians 5:25, Paul equates love to giving. He says that the purpose of giving is to open the receiver's heart in order to remove what is not from God. This means: When God gives, He takes what is of Himself and He deposits it in a person who would receive Him. 2 Timothy 1:7 says that God gave us His Spirit to birth love within us. The sanctifying effect of God's Spirit in our inner being causes us to begin to love and give to others. When this takes place, it is a true reflection of a change taking place within a person. Giving something of themselves out of love demonstrates a removal of selfishness and has a profound effect on the receiver. Love is shed abroad in their hearts and they in turn give to others. Giving is a godly attribute that is duplicated in the life of the receiver.

In Matthew 10 Jesus sends out His disciples with the message of the arrival of the Kingdom of God. It is in the context of this passage that Jesus says in verse 8 that His Kingdom is a giving Kingdom. He gives it to the disciples for free and they are to receive it as such and give it away at no cost. Jesus paid the price as He gave Himself for us and we as the receivers should give it away as we have received it – for free. The Kingdom of God is a gift to all those who would receive it.

Act of worship

A gift does not come without boundaries. When we receive the gift of life from God, we are required to reciprocate God's gift by giving Him our lives in return as living sacrifices. This is what Paul explains to us in Romans 12:1. Paul calls this kind of giving our act of worship to God. If we truly understand the gift of God, the sacrifice of His Son as a propitiation for our sins, we will respond to it with all our being. The gift of a Saviour dying for us on the cross was never meant to give us a licence to live a life apart from God, nor a life without any restraints. The ultimate intention of God's gift to us, Christ as the sacrificial lamb, was to reconcile us back into a relationship with Him. Within this relationship God gives us parameters that sustain our devotion to Him.

God's blessing, His gift to His people of the Old Testament Israel was His presence among them. In the New Testament, His gift is Jesus Christ dying on the cross, which allowed for the Spirit of God to come and indwell every believer. No greater gift can any person receive, than God Himself making His home within the heart of the believer. God's gift to us is a person, not an object that resembles Him, nor a set of rules or laws. Unfortunately, people have exchanged love for the person of God with a love for the guidelines God gave. This law-observance removes all love and elevates self-centred fleshly boasting.

Christianity is unlike other religions in that it is based on a personal relationship with the living God. This relationship is initiated the gift that comes from God through the sacrificial death of His Son. All other religions have their laws, regulations and commandments as the focus of their devotion, but relationships cannot exist between a person and a set of rules. All it can do is inform a person about their imperfections. When we develop a true relationship with God, we experience true fulfilment and joy.

Love spawns giving and giving in turn demonstrates love, which creates a spiral of giving. When we begin to understand the length and breadth of the gift of God to us, we, in turn, begin giving back to God by giving to others. This was Paul's message to the churches. He encouraged them to give to one another and uses several instances where he speaks of Christ giving Himself to us. In Ephesians 5 he says Christ gave Himself up for us as a fragrant offering and a sacrifice to God. In 1 Timothy 2:6, Paul says Christ gave Himself as a ransom for all. Paul uses the example of Jesus and how He gave Himself for the church to encourage husbands to give themselves to their wives as an expression of their spousal love.

Giving of goods, our time and knowledge are different to giving of oneself. When wealthy people give of their wealth to the poor, it is not as elevated as when someone gives their life as a sacrifice for others. No greater love, Jesus says in John 15:13, can exist than when someone lays down their life for the sake of others. Self-sacrifice is opposite to selfishness. The former is of divine origin, while the latter is of the devil.

No other gift in history can explain grace better than God's plan of salvation. It details God's unmerited favour deposited like rain upon a desert-like scorched earth. It was the greatest gift given to a non-deserving people and it surpasses human thinking. Jesus' last words on the cross showed that in order to reconcile us back to Himself, God the Father turned His face away from His own Son. The gift God gave this world demonstrated what God views as the most important thing in His eyes – the relationship He desires with every believer.

Creation has God's signature all over it. It is a grandiose display of a Creator's giving of Himself. After God created a beautiful

245

garden, He did two important things. Firstly, He formed mankind from dust and gave Himself to mankind. Secondly, God gave custody of the garden, which was His, to mankind. Giving shows love, an action which flows out of God's loving nature. We can see that the principle of giving of ourselves, like God did, is something we need to emulate. God Himself affords us the power to also create love in the hearts of others when we give. Jesus instructed people to "give and it shall be given unto you", "sow and you shall reap" and "plant and you will see a harvest". Giving and sowing unleash the power of God's creational law of seed-bearing – it is undeniable.

Jesus' birth is remembered every year when we give gifts to each other in the same manner as the wise men from the east gave gifts to the baby Jesus. When men give gold, frankincense and myrrh to someone, they demonstrate that nothing should stop us from giving to others.

Giving within a relationship can be tangible or intangible. Giving tangible gifts is slightly easier than giving intangible gifts. Generally, a good indicator of the maturity of a relationship is the level of giving that takes place. Gary Chapman has done an excellent job in his book, *The Five Love Languages*. He details five 'languages' through which love, within a marriage relationship, can be expressed, and interestingly, only two of the five ways are tangible. The rest are intangible ways of selfless giving. Some of these intangible ways can be seen in the level of grace spouses afford each other, like forgiveness, sacrificial acts of service, unconditional acceptance, which are signs indicating the growth and depth of a relationship.

Chapter 24

Always be on your guard

I f we look at the nature and consequence of sin, we can see that it is designed to bring division and separation. Whether it separates people from each other or people from God, sin always separates. It is the greatest enemy of any relationship. When sin shows up, hidden within a certain temptation, its evil intention doesn't show its face. If it did, I believe we would recognise it and walk away from it. But sin hides within a situation designed by the devil to lure, trick and divide.

The Genesis 3 account is a crystal-clear example of how the devil drove a wedge between God and man. The ripple-effect in Genesis 4 showed a wedge between people. A powerful teaching by the late Doctor Michael Eaton (2017) taught us as believers to be on our guard against temptation. The focus of his teaching was to inform believers and non-believers regarding the reason why God created mankind. His teaching also focused on the reason why mankind, in their current state, were not reconciled to God. Dr Eaton's "Temptation-Investigation" method equips believers to look behind the curtain and not be blinded by the smoke and mirrors, and to always check our thoughts, motives and surroundings whenever we discern temptation coming our way. This world offers many temptations to stir our lust for what our eyes desire – things with which we cannot build a relationship. God uses transparent gold as paving in heaven, which tells us that to God, possessions serve a functional purpose, and in John 3:16, Scripture shows that to God, relationships are most valuable.

Another important aspect we must remember is that every relationship has boundaries that are like the walls of a city, the doors of a home, the government of a country, and the laws of nature. These boundaries keep us safe. Whether we discuss marriages, friendships, business dealings or partnerships, the health of any relationship depends on the honouring of the boundaries governing that specific relationship. These boundaries also govern the relationship between God and mankind, and should they be allowed to collapse, the relationships will collapse. Within the scope of these boundaries, we find aspects such as respect, being considerate, authority, kindness, self-control, selflessness, gentleness and many others, as the foundation stones of healthy relationships.

The saying that 'familiarity breeds contempt' is so true. In the Bible we see how Paul not only instructed Timothy in ways to effectively communicate Scripture, but he also instructed him to maintain respect within the church community between the different age groups. For instance, in 1 Timothy 5:1, he instructs Timothy to respect older people. Whenever a younger person loses respect for an older person, people lose respect for the younger person. When a relationship is taken for granted or one of the parties betrays the mutual respect, the relationship enters stormy waters. A healthy relationship requires both parties to maintain an awareness of the boundaries in their relationship, even if the boundaries are not clearly stipulated from the beginning.

Relational boundaries are there to ensure that other important aspects needed for a healthy relationship, are maintained. These can include mutual respect, forgiveness, honesty, trust, clear communication, good listening skills, intentional investment in time, and many others. An aspect I want to highlight, is respect. Respect is a deep admiration for someone's abilities, achievements and qualities, and if we are to maintain healthy relationships, we need to maintain healthy levels of mutual respect.

If we as believers have developed a healthy relationship with the Trinity, as Scripture teaches us, we will be in a good position to develop and maintain healthy relationships with other people. This applies to non-believers, work colleagues, spouses and neighbours. The focus of this book is that God is interested in developing a personal relationship with every person who seeks Him.

Proverbs 18:24 says that God is our friend who sticks closer than a brother. Scripture invites us to seek after God (Jeremiah 29:13; 1 Chronicles 16:11; Proverbs 8:7; Acts 17:27; Hebrews 11:6). How do we know we are seeking after Him? Well, Scripture is clear that we do not seek after God out of our own will. We do so because He draws us. God draws those He calls and He enables them to respond. This response then gives rise to a relationship with God which lasts forever. This is the essence of the Gospel – not that we believe just in order to escape the flames, but that we respond to the call of God to become His friends.

An important aspect I want to highlight here is how we are to view our relationship with God. The correct view of God will ensure an ever-deepening relationship with Him. Ecclesiastes 5:2

says we should always be on our guard when approaching God, warning us to always remain humble before God and remember who we are and who God is. "Do not be quick with your mouth, do not be hasty in your heart to utter anything before God. God is in heaven and you are on earth, so let your words be few" (NIV). Those who have ignored this warning have suffered greatly.

Familiarity, by preachers and teachers, when using Scripture, causes misunderstanding in the lives of believers (Isaiah 66:2). When it comes to the Holy Spirit of God, familiarity causes Him to step back and withdraw. God the Father is the potter and we are the clay; not the other way around (Jeremiah 18). Proverbs also instructs us to revere God. The author says to revere God is the beginning of wisdom and understanding (Proverbs 1:7). Training ourselves to be on our guard regarding the boundaries within our relationships will ensure the health and longevity of the relationships.

Nicodemus's story

Here is a short factual anecdote of a man who gave up everything to follow Jesus. He was a prominent leader in Jerusalem who met Jesus in person and became convinced that Jesus was who He said He was. He was one of the camels who managed to pass through the eye of a needle (Matthew 19:24). His story is an encourage-ment to many believers who have progressed to places of promi-nence and wealth in this life and, in many cases, have become trapped by their positions and wealth and feel unable to publicly demonstrate their faith in Jesus for fear of being victimised. The man I am referring to was the leader of the Jewish Sanhedrin, the most powerful legal body and the final authority on decision-making concerning Jewish religious and political life. He was the

Pharisee, Nicodemus, who visited Jesus at night (John 3). In John 3:10 Jesus Himself acknowledged Nicodemus as, "The teacher of Israel," proof of his public status and profile.

This man's story demonstrates how important it is to have a long-term view that transcends this life. The depth of the relationship we are able to develop with Jesus in this life has a great impact on the life to come. Similarly, if we live for the praise of the masses, we will inevitably forego our friendship with God.

To the majority of nations in Jesus' times, burial sites were an important aspect. They said much about who was buried there and the person's wealth and status in society. While the wealthy prepared lavish graves for themselves, others like the poor, despised lepers and those executed were buried in what were known as 'common graves' because of a lack of funds to purchase a burial site, or as a sign of humiliation or contempt.

In John 19:38-39 we see Joseph of Arimathea, another prominent man, who approached Pilate for the body of Jesus. He was joined by Nicodemus who brought a large quantity of spices to embalm Jesus' body. It was a significant event for a Pharisee – not so much taking care of a body but taking care of the body of Jesus – a man despised and killed by the Jewish Council. Nicodemus's action was similar to that of Mary Magdalene (John 12:7). Both sacrificed their finances and humbled themselves publicly in the sight of God.

Nicodemus was one of the Jewish leaders who, by his association with Jesus, lost all worldly wealth and position. Sources outside Scripture say Nicodemus's remains were found in a common grave next to the remains of Stephen, the martyr in Acts 6. Also found in the same common grave were the remains of Gamaliel, a leading authority in the Jewish Sanhedrin. He was the Jewish leader who stepped in on behalf of the apostles in Acts 5:33-39 who chose to obey God rather than men. Nicodemus was believed to have been saved before Jesus' death, and the Sanhedrin made sure he retained no position of power, possessions or prominence. Despite the certainty of loss, he became a believer and demonstrated that following Christ was worth it all.

Insurance or assurance

Some of the earlier passages in this book have detailed how God views us as worth it all to send His all to save us all. Once we realise the extent to which He went to rescue us and bring us back into a relationship with Himself, we become willing to give Him our all. This is the only thing worth giving ourselves and our lives to. To God, we were worth it all. It is worth our all to respond to His love.

Reading through Scripture for many years, preparing teachings and preaches, I have experienced a drawing of my heart to a friendship and fellowship with God more and more. From one level of intimacy to the next, and to another ever-increasing desire to know our great God better, know He will not stop at anything to restore His family back to Himself.

John wrote about our assurance of our eternal destiny. In John 17:2, John quotes Jesus saying that eternal life is received from the Father through Himself. He has been given the authority to deposit divine life within a person. In verse 3, Jesus says eternal life is equated to knowing God. This means that every person who enters a relationship with God begins to live a life infused with divine power. This is God's life given to a person to empower them to know God. It opens the person's eyes of their heart to understand God better, to walk in His ways and it allows for dialogue between God and the person. This life begins when a person places their faith in the sacrificial death of Jesus.

This is what we understand as the initial process called justification in the salvation process of the believer. Uninformed believers can act like Paul's superstitious audience in Acts 17:22-24. They had manmade gods in their temples. They feared the gods and would rather try and appease them all rather than fall into judgement by omitting one god, so they added a god they called "An unknown god" as insurance against being judged.

Paul explained to the crowd that it is God who gives life and breath to all – something only God can give. From verses 27-31, Paul explains more about God's intentions for mankind, that God created mankind to be dependent on their Creator, to seek after Him, and to be in a loving relationship with Him. God does not want to be seen as distant or absent from what He created, which was a theme Paul addressed when he spoke in Athens in Acts 17.

What does the "guarantee" in 2 Corinthians 1:22 refer to? "Now it is God who makes both us and you stand firm in Christ. He anointed us, set his seal of ownership on us, and put His Spirit in our hearts as a deposit, guaranteeing what is to come" (NIV). To understand what Paul means, we need to read 2 Corinthians 1:4-6. Here Paul speaks about a certain "comfort" God is to the believer and John describes the Spirit of God as the "Comforter". In 2 Corinthians 1:21-22, Paul says God's Eternal Spirit makes the believer stand firm when He enters the believer's heart. It cements the believer's identity when God puts His seal of ownership on the believer. The guarantee that Paul refers to is a 'knowing' deep inside the heart of the believer, which develops with time. As years go by, the believer's trust in God grows. It is not a trust based on the believer's ability or works, but based on the witness from the eternal Spirit Himself within our hearts. He is responsible for the assurance or confidence that develops within the believer. He convicts the believer of sin and if the believer's faith is put into action, He also convicts the believer of righteousness. This is the assurance we have of our eternal relationship with God.

It becomes clear that the "guarantee" Paul refers to can only be received through the eternal Spirit of God who renews the mind of the believer to accept God's initiation towards the restoration of fellowship. It is not possible for a person to relate to God or have any means of fellowship with God without the Spirit of God facilitating such a friendship. In Romans 8:7, Paul says the mind of a person without the Spirit of God is "hostile" to God, and that those who have the Spirit of God "belong" to God. Belonging to God is the establishment of an eternal bond, which God, through His Spirit's presence in the heart of the believer, guarantees. What God deposits, He does not withdraw by His will.

In Romans 8:11, Paul explains more about the guarantee we receive when God's Spirit comes to dwell in the heart of the believer. This guarantee takes place at the point of justification, meaning when the Spirit comes to settle in the heart of the believer. This guarantee, also described as a deposit or down-payment by God, becomes the believer's assurance of eternal life and of their friendship with God while in their decaying earthly body. Although it might take the believer a long time to heed the voice and leading of the Spirit of God within, it is at the point of justification by grace through faith that when the believer's relationship with God turns from hostility to friendship.

Paul explains in Romans 8:11 how the resurrection of Christ is the turning point. When mankind was granted the ability, through Christ's death, burial and resurrection, to receive the eternal Spirit of God as a permanent Friend who comes to inhabit the heart of every believer. The eternal Spirit of God testifies in our hearts to the hope we have of being God's children for ever.

Not only does the Spirit of God show that the process of salvation in the heart of the believer has begun, it is also a guarantee of what God started in the life of the believer, He will finish. The resurrection of Christ was and still is the hinge doctrine in salvation that guarantees our hope of eternal life after death. This life afforded by the Spirit of God, is more powerful than the first death, also known as man's natural death.

Easier said than grasped is the fact that God's Spirit in us is the presence of God in us. It is our guarantee against the second death, also known as eternal separation from God. It is the Spirit of God who raised Christ from the grave. We will also be raised from the grave to immortal life if He indwells us as He did Christ. If He indwells us, His presence overrides the sting of death at the point of our justification.

Another way the Spirit's presence in us is a guarantee of what God will do in future is mentioned in Romans 8:6. Paul says that the mind governed by the Spirit is life and peace. This God-given peace (John 20:21) is similar to the comfort Paul mentions in 2 Corinthians 1:4-6. The indwelling Spirit of God fills the believer with a peace that develops within the believer through the friendship the believer has with His Saviour. This God-given peace triumphs over all adversity and uncertainty. It is a peace directly from the Spirit of Christ (2 Thessalonians 3:16). It comforts the believer in suffering and assures him of all God has promised.

The promise God made was that the same Sprit who factually raised Christ from the dead will also raise the believer (Romans 8:11). This promise is conditional; verse 11 uses the word "if" which refers to the condition that the Spirit of God must indwell the believer. It is by means of the fulfilment of this condition that the guarantee is effective and available to the believer.

Despite claims by Islam, Buddhism, Hinduism and many other religions, there exists no other 'vehicle' available or claim that any adherent can make, apart from the gift of the indwelling Spirit, that gives the assurance of being raised to life and fellowship with God after death. This promise by God keeps the believer the whole way and beyond death. It is a guarantee, made by God Himself, afforded to every believer.

In Romans 8:14-15, Paul mentions two very interesting words. He speaks of sonship and adoption. He is referring to all believers who have the Spirit of God dwelling in them and facilitating eternal fellowship between God and the believer. Paul's remarks are life changing. He states that those who follow the Spirit's lead are no longer servants but adopted sons. The free gift of God's grace extends to every believer allowing them to become co-heirs with His Son Jesus. There is a closer relational bond than that of a father-son relationship. Jesus and the Father are one (John 10:30). Therefore, through God's gracious act of adoption, we have been given the right to become as close to God as His own Son Jesus. The astounding effect of having been given sonship is that it guarantees and secures the believer's identity and future. People can undo contracts they have signed and they can go back on their promises. But no person, power, ruler, empirical scientific finding or even death can undo our sonship and being co-heirs with Christ. This is an eternal position we are given through Christ in God.

Insurance is a guarantee of compensation against a specified loss that will be given by a company for a monetary exchange – depending on the full disclosure of the risk related to the specified potential loss. Insurance cover gives people a level of peace of mind that the particular asset has been covered should anything happen to it. When compared with Scripture, this is not what God intended for those who believe in Him. God's intention is not a contractual insurance policy that can be cancelled. His intention from the start was an assurance, a personal relationship guaranteeing our eternal resting place with Him. God did not contract with us. He covenanted with us in His own blood and swore in His own name to be faithful.

The way to become assured is by knowing beyond the shadow of a doubt what your destiny is after death. Your eternal destiny becomes clear and assured through the relationship you have entered into with the Person of Jesus. The level of trust you have developed over time, the time you have invested, and the understanding you have gained of who God is, results in a personal relationship with Him. You have placed all control into the hands of God. This intimate relationship you have built with the Father, through His Son Jesus and by the help of the Spirit is the strongest connection with God available to man. This relationship is the guarantee of God's constant presence – His provision and protection while we walk this earth. The NIV version of the John 3:16 says: "Whoever believes..." in the present perfect tense and in the singular form, addressing every single believer who puts their trust in God.

During testing times of danger, David wrote in Psalm 61:2 that God is his rock, the rock that is higher than himself. The reassurance we have is that no one has to be their own assurance or guarantee. We do not have to strive to save ourselves from the mess this world is in because of sin. We do not have to risk our all to gain anything. God is our assurance and in Him we rest.

When a person's assurance of their salvation in God becomes real for them, an amazing occurrence for a convert is that they become secure in their identity. This is a powerful step forward and they are secure in who God is in them and who they are in God. The relationship, which has led to their assurance, now gives rise to a humble, yet confident stance before God. This is not because of who they are or what they have accomplished, but who they are joined to and represented by. Jesus has become the 'Big Brother' of every believer. He secures their future and empowers their present. The believer now moves forward and begins to understand that they do not have to 'perform' or convince others of their status before God, nor is there any need for them to win God's favour through their human attempts of being 'good enough'. They know that they are loved by their Father in heaven, and a father's love is worth more than all the gold, silver and prestige in this world (see Matthew 3:17).

Chapter 25

One sacrifice for all for ever

In this chapter, I want to touch on the part sacrifices play in any relationship. Of all the creatures God created, mankind is the only one God has a relationship with. Previously I discussed how human beings brought sin into this world. Mankind was therefore exclusively responsible for the relational breakdown between himself and God. The remedy for sin had to come from God who is sinless and pure. A single, once and for all sacrifice was required to pay for the sin of all of mankind. One scapegoat would pay the price, be the ransom, which would reunite man to God.

As mentioned previously, sin brings division and separation and either prevents or destroys relationships known to God and mankind. How can sin and its destructive effects on relationships be halted? Well, through the act of a single sacrifice, once for all, for ever (Hebrews 10:10), God Himself declared it to be the only legal way to remove the nature and consequence of sin. While the giver of the sacrifice pays a price, the receiver benefits from it and receives life and freedom. Throughout Scripture, the principle of a sacrifice remains as a hinge for many Biblical principles and doctrines.

A sacrifice that is birthed in love is the wilful act of a person who chooses to become less so that the other person can become more. A sacrifice ends all selfishness because it is rooted in 1 Corinthians 13 love. It promotes the wellbeing and welfare of others and it glorifies God as the original 'Giver'. A sacrifice demonstrates wisdom by not holding onto something, but rather sowing it to reap a future reward.

In the context of relationships, one sacrifice or the gift of forgiveness, covers or removes the contention between two parties in order to restore the fellowship. The Old Testament account of the Day of Atonement (Leviticus 16) is a clear example of how an innocent scapegoat is sacrificed for the sake of many under judgement. It represents one life given to save the lives of others. The Leviticus 16 day was the foreshadow of the day Jesus would die on the cross to make atonement for mankind's sin.

Any conflict in a relationship has to do with one person being dishonoured in some way. Satan is the author of broken relationships and the instigator of distrust and disunity. The powerful weapon he wields against relationships is to influence people into becoming self-centred. This causes the breakdown of the relational bond. Satan did this in Genesis 3:1-5 and succeeded in separating mankind from God. His influence was seen immediately after this in Genesis 4 when Cain killed his brother Abel. Evil is visible in the ugly seeds of hate, disunity and suspicion. This eventually breaks apart the relationship, leaving a trail of destruction, distrust and broken promises. Selfishness, in most cases, is the face of the third person who gets between two people in a relationship. A sacrifice made in the right way at the right moment ushers in a level of authority. It is a Godly principle that demonstrates the power of God's Spirit opposing the spirit of disunity, strife and selfishness. Love always triumphs over evil. When a sacrifice is made in a relationship, it stirs the other person to reciprocate the love expressed through the initial sacrifice, and when this happens, the relationship matures to a deeper level.

An integral part of a sacrifice is the aspect of testing. If a gift does not cost the giver anything, it is not a sacrifice. The greater the cost, the more impact the sacrifice will have. A true sacrifice is costly and requires the trust provided by a relationship before it is given. The test, which accompanies a sacrifice, is the ability to overcome an inherent fear in the mind of the giver that their giving will not be honoured.

A sacrifice is also volitional and can never be forced. In Jesus' own words to the Pharisees: "I lay down my life willingly" (John 10:18). A sacrifice can be suggested, but it still requires the giver to give it. A sacrifice is costly on the part of the one making the sacrifice, yet at the same time it is received freely by the recipient. The impact is that although one person pays the price, both benefit from the gift. A gift, when given to a deserving person is merely a gift. But when given to a non-deserving person, it is called a grace-gift, which is given with clear relational intentions. Why would someone give a gift to an enemy if the giver does not expect a change in the receiver's status from enemy to friend? It is this intention God displayed when giving His Son as a ransom for all. God willingly gave His Son to stir our hearts to reciprocate His love. God's hand was never forced into making a sacrifice. He did it out of love for the people He created.

Many Biblical references draw our attention to the power of a sacrifice to either establish a relationship or heal it. As long as the partners in any relationship continue a sacrificial attitude of the heart, the relationship will be healthy. A sacrificial heart loves practically and gives with understanding; it is a heart that honours their neighbour more than themselves. A sacrificial heart is a heart after God's heart of giving, blessing, restoring and loving.

God gave Abraham the test of his life by asking him to sacrifice his only son – the son of promise (Genesis 22). By obeying God's request, Abraham showed his understanding of the value of his relationship with God. The son he loved, who carried the hope of Israel's existence, was less important than his relationship with God.

The woman at Solomon's feet (1 Kings 3:16-27) demonstrated how she would sacrifice the 'ownership' of her child to ensure he stays alive. She was willing to lose what was dear to her to preserve the life of her baby. A sacrificial heart gives up temporal pleasures for the sake of life-long benefits.

One for all means one price paid will cover the wrongs of an entire world (John 11:49-51). God applied this principle over the entire world when His Son died for the sins of all of mankind. Jesus became the Lamb who was slain to take away the sins of this world.

After Adam and Eve fell into sin, God Himself sacrificed an animal to provide a skin to cover humanity's nakedness (Genesis 3:21).

Esther risked her life to save the Jews targeted by the wicked Haman (Esther 5:2-4).

One of the best ways to begin the restoration of a relationship is with the words, "I am sorry." A sacrifice is a sign of the Spirit of God working within a person's heart. His Spirit softens both hearts to give up the position they had held onto and receive what they could not before. The evidence of the fellowshipping Spirit of God is seen in the love, joy and peace at work between the parties.

Chapter 26

The solid hope I stand on

Atheists do not acknowledge God and by doing so, they ignore the existence of love. Without love, people become suspicious of everyone else. In the absence of love, no one can be trusted. Love gives hope because of the relationship and trust springing forth from love. For the atheist, the absence of hope brings an anxiety about the future. They have no hinge of faith to attach their door to and no foundation for their theories. Atheists often want to argue with Christians against God, yet they have nothing like Christianity's relationship with God to put forward.

An individual living without God will in most cases point a finger at something else – usually the finger is pointed at the church. The church is made up of normal people who are not perfect, they have been declared righteous before God for putting their faith in His plan of dealing with their sin.

What is the solid hope I stand on? What does hope look like in the middle of a storm? What is the link between my life on this earth and the life to come?

My solid foundation is my relationship with God. It is the thread, which Jesus mentioned in John 17:3, of knowing the Father. Knowing God is not a scientific element nor can He be measured scientifically. It is a deep inward knowing that God who we trust and worship, is faithful. He has proven Himself over and over. No person, argument or an unpleasant single event can disprove the goodness of God. As one person said to me on their deathbed: "I know that I know He loves me." This is the hope we have. It is our connectedness to God that transfers us into the life to come. It drives away all fear, anxiety and suspicion. Our relationship with God is our solid hope that when we close our eyes in this world, we open them up in heaven.

What the Father values most

What any father values most is to see his children live in peace with each other. No father can command unity in his family. Unity is a precious attribute that is only developed over time. Unity cannot be bought or downloaded from the internet. Unity in any relationship is the outcome when both parties in the relationship have had their hearts circumcised by the Spirit of God. Like faith, unity among brothers attracts God's attention. When He finds it He blesses it (Psalm 133:1-3).

The Bible begins and ends with a friendship within the Trinity and a friendship between God and the people of His pasture, and a key focus throughout is on relationships. Pivotal to this key focus is God the Father who is over everything and everyone (1 Corinthians 15:24). Scripture portrays God as a Father, which means He shows Himself as someone within a family. This close relationship is what gave birth to humanity in Genesis 1:26. From this relationship, all other relationships developed. God is life and if He is found within the relationships, then life flows through the relationships. It is here where growth, expansion, wellness, fruitfulness and abundance emanate from.

We begin to understand the importance of relationships when we listen to Jesus speaking on the Father's behalf in John 12:49. Again in Matthew chapters 5-7, we are taught to lay aside all other distractions, worldly pursuits and worries to build what has eternal value which Jesus showed was our relationship with God and our neighbour (Matthew 6:19-21).

If relationships are one of the things the Father values most, then relationships will be one of the aspects we will be judged by. In Matthew 22:37-40, Jesus said that all the Law and the Prophets are summed up by two commandments. Jesus highlights what is of greatest importance to the Father – Love, which is the greatest commandment, expressed towards God and secondly towards our neighbour, found in relationships.

What we need to remember is that love is not a subject on its own. Love is found in a relationship. Love does not create relationships. Relationships create true love. Nowhere in Scripture is love expressed as a lone-standing idea or principle. Galatians 5:21 states that love is the first fruit of the Spirit of God. Love is therefore the result of a relationship, not the origin of it. Love cannot exist without more than one person. For this reason, love cannot be found in any other religion or belief-system, but only in the Trinity of the Father, Son and Holy Spirit. Here love is expressed in its purest form. It is not surprising that Jesus says that love, which is synonymous with relationships, is the one thing that sums up all the Law and the Prophets.

Love, as Jesus explains it in John 14:15, is an expression of humble reverent obedience and honour towards God. Love, between people, remains an expression of our reverence and honour for God. There exists no greater worth, no greater pursuit, no greater achievement, and no greater resource than a relationship that gives birth to love. To experience lasting love, we need to maintain a lasting relationship.

God with us – God for us – God within us

Perhaps we have been caught up in arguments about issues in Scripture and, while we make connections between various verses contained in the Bible, trying to prove our own interpretations of Scripture, we have missed the most important message from God. There are events in Scripture when God was not whispering. No, in fact, He was trumpeting His message from the mountain tops.

An example could be a mother of three cooking dinner, but because of persistent fighting and arguing by the children, the mother gets distracted and burns the food. It is the same with us when studying Scripture. We so easily get distracted by the detail, the language and the history that can we miss out on the most important aspect, which is the message from the author. Jesus Himself warned the Pharisees about this issue (John 5:39-40).

Scripture details God's plan to dwell with His people. Unfortunately, we either take this for granted so often or we argue about how and with who He is going to do this. Furthermore, the busyness of life and the demands placed upon us from a young age, have the effect that we run out of time to spend time with God. If God wanted to give us more time, He would not have limited our daylight hours to twelve and expected us to also sleep.

The reason God took on the body of a man explains a significant difference between the Old and the New Testament. Matthew

1:23 says Jesus will be called, "Emmanuel," meaning, "God with us." In the Old Testament God was seen in many different expressions and forms. Israel saw Him as a dark cloud, as lightening, the voice speaking to them, a column of fire, and in many other ways. They were not allowed to see God or they would die.

Jesus' incarnation signified a major relational shift compared to what Israel experienced. God accompanied them with His presence, but He did not indwell them. We see how God dwelt with Israel and its leaders. God was with His people. He fought their wars and provided all they needed. Yet, God could only come and dwell among their tents and then had to leave again. The reason for this 'distant relationship' was because mankind's sin was not yet completely atoned for.

With Jesus' arrival in the New Testament, the change began. Through the prophets, God foretold a time would come when He would indwell His people (Jeremiah 32:38-39). It would only be after the New Covenant had been sealed in Jesus' blood that the penalty for sin could be paid once and forever (Hebrews 10:14). By dying on the cross and being resurrected, Jesus paid the full price to purchase righteousness on man's behalf. Jesus fulfilled the righteous requirements of the Law and through this, God could establish a holy people for Himself.

Jesus' death on the cross, His burial, His resurrection, and His ascension paved the way for the Holy Spirit to arrive as promised by Jesus. The curtain of separation between God and mankind has forever been removed and God could indwell man. The tabernacle of God was no longer a manmade tent, a building, nor a temple among His people. God's tabernacle was the people of God themselves (2 Corinthians 6:16). Under the Old Covenant,

God was with and for His people. Now, under the New Covenant, God is in His people.

God's plan of salvation has been the means designed to accomplish His eternal goal of positioning Himself firstly with, then among, and finally within His people.

No other religion, no other creature, no other ideology has what we as Christians have – God the Creator of everything and everyone, dwelling in us. No person can boast that they have achieved this. God Himself gave Himself to dwell within us. It is truly worth it all to pursue and understand God's plan of fellowship with mankind.

A final point to ponder

I am from an area on the southern tip of Africa where the world's richest deposits of precious minerals are found. Companies who have mining rights create incredible wealth for their international shareholders. The socio-economic development, albeit skew in terms of the distribution of wealth, is remarkable. People from around the world relocate to work and earn a better living here. Yet, these precious minerals are finite commodities. These minerals have a huge impact on people's social development and wellbeing, but they cannot be a source of hope. Although they are the lifeblood to many businesses in the area, they will eventually run out.

So many people place their hopes in finite items such as these minerals. They work their whole lives just to see their entire life savings evaporate as the world's financial markets and systems collapse. What do we take with us when we die?

Imagine you are liquidated, like Job was in Job 1:11-12, and every single item is taken away from you – even the clothes on your body. Naked you come into this world and naked you shall leave (Job 1:21). This Scripture speaks of every earthly thing we collect and horde. The only thing we do take with us beyond the grave is the relationship we have built with God the Father, the Son, and the Holy Spirit. This relationship is the believer's assurance, his eternal inheritance, his guarantee of eternal salvation.

This is our eternal Promised Land. When we, who have walked with God, close our eyes here on earth, we will open them in the presence of our best Friend (John 5:28). Why do we get so distracted and waste time building worthless empires? We should spend our time investing in our eternal friendship with God, which is our guaranteed assurance.

Finally, Paul puts it plainly in Romans 8:18. He says that only children can be heirs of God, referring to a family relationship. This means we are to be born of God, born of the Spirit of God, just like Jesus was (Luke 1:35), into the family of God. This makes every believer a co-heir with Christ. To inherit His all will require my all. God enables us to an investment from our side to share in both Christ's sufferings and His glory. This investment is worth it all.

To conclude

It is hard to write on the all-encompassing subject of the loving relationship God has invited us into. In the end, we can say with certainty that there is something worth more than all the possessions, prominence, power, money and positions in this world. And there is so much more for every believer than just getting saved. Once we open our hearts to Him drawing us to Himself, He touches our hearts, and from this moment on we are able to share in an eternal relationship, a friendship with the God of all life and love. Within this relationship we find true joy, fulfilment, peace, acceptance and love. In the words of Christian author, Peter Jeffrey, "All the gifts of God are for us to enjoy, but the greatest pleasure is to enjoy God Himself."

God with us, God for us and God in us. This is the most incredible and gracious gift God has bestowed upon us. God Himself has come to abide within us to be our Helper in all things. With the help of the Spirit of Fellowship, we want to do what pleases God. It is an obedience born from a renewed heart that does not have its origin within our reasoning. God, by His Spirit, helps us to see things the way He sees them. He guides our hearts minute-by-minute to walk in step with Him. His wisdom becomes ours. The Spirit is the only one who can fulfil the heart of God because He is the only one Who truly knows the heart of God. He opens our eyes to see where we are tempted to exchange worthless worldly pursuits for time spent in the presence of the eternal God. God's Spirit indwelling us has sealed us into an eternal relationship with our Creator, our Father, our Saviour and our Lord.

When all is said and done, it is not the knowledge, the possessions and fame we have accumulated, it is our relationship with God through Christ that is the deciding factor. Our obedience to God is the aspect through which our love and devotion to God are demonstrated. God Himself initiated the step to reconcile us to Himself. He gave His all to save us all. It is worth looking past the distractions this world offers us so we can focus on what lies ahead. Difficulties will come and we will experience setbacks, but because we have God as our friend, we can conquer it all. God's loving friendship is truly worth it all.

About the Author

The author has been serving as a pastor in various pastoral roles since the age of eighteen and is currently serving in the Pentecostal Holiness Church in Phokeng, near the town of Rustenburg in the North-West Province, South Africa. The author has been involved in producing educational material for discipleship training programs and courses to train aspiring preachers and teachers in the local church. The denominational church affiliation the author is currently serving in, has its roots in the 1909 Azusa Street Revival in the USA. The current church in its African setting has a global reach into many countries and continents.

The author is trained as a chartered accountant and holds a post-graduate degree in Theology. He has extensive experience in both the corporate world and church missions. Having travelled extensively, the author has a fair understanding of diverse cultures in and outside the church. He has also studied how other religions stand up to the true Gospel of Christ. Part of the author's research and passion is to understand the Theological basis and practical outworking of the relationship between God and mankind. Over many years the author has devoted time and energy to help believers in the church to know God better. It is the author's resolve to see believers invest their time, energy and talents in what is of eternal worth, compared to temporary worldly happiness. It is the author's deep conviction that God has something amazing in store for every believer, which goes much further than just being saved from their sin. The author's work will draw the believer's attention to God's true intention regarding their salvation.

It has been the author's personal journey to seek and understand why God wants to reconcile people to Himself. As a person actively involved in managing a family business, the author has seen and experienced both the lure and the deceitfulness of worldly wealth. The author has seen God involve Himself in his personal life, causing him to ask: Is there perhaps something more to the average Christian life we are missing out on?

www.ingramcontent.com/pod-product-compliance
Lightning Source LLC
Chambersburg PA
CBHW060206070426
42447CB00034B/2700